SUCCESSFUL INVESTING IN STAMPS AND BANKNOTES

SUCCESSFUL INVESTING IN STAMPS AND BANKNOTES

By Colin Narbeth and David Lyon of Stanley Gibbons Limited
Catalogue of Early English Banks by James Douglas

Graham & Trotman Limited Publishers
20 Foubert's Place
Regent Street
London W1V 1HH

First published 1975 in Great Britain by Graham & Trotman Limited, Publishers, 20 Foubert's Place, Regent Street, London W1V 1HH

Printed by Redwood Burn Ltd. of Trowbridge and Esher
Designed by Patrick Frean

Graham & Trotman Limited Publishers

ISBN 0 86010 007 3

CONTENTS

FOREWORD

by John Webb of STANLEY GIBBONS LTD

Within months of the first adhesive postage stamps being issued in 1840, people were collecting them. Collectors have grown in number ever since. Stamp collecting is without doubt the largest collecting hobby in the world. Having stood the test of time for more than 130 years it is clear that they must be a good investment. It is difficult to know what motivates a collector but I can say that so long as people collect, stamps will always be in the forefront.

It is not a simple matter to invest in stamps. There are many stamps that do not appreciate much in value even though they may give immense pleasure to collectors. This book sets out to illustrate the type of stamps which are most likely to go up in value. The investor can see for himself the upward trend of prices and the sometimes quite enormous jumps in value. It is perhaps significant that the most valuable item in the world for its size and weight is a postage stamp. It will always pay serious investors to always seek advice from the major dealers in the world like Stanley Gibbons Limited, who run a special investors' service.

Experience has shown that about fifty per cent of those who start out as investors turn into collectors. That in itself demonstrates the strength of the hobby. Why is it so attractive? Stamps don't take up much room — a million pounds worth can be housed in one album in a bookshelf; they don't weigh much and are easy to carry; they can be beautiful works of art, teach history and geography and unfold the story of the posts which, after all was vital for the development of the civilised world. Fast communication was essential for the growth of commerce and indeed for nations at war. An investment portfolio of stamps can be an interesting talking point and display to show friends as well as a means of saving for the future.

Nor should the investor neglect the field of rare banknotes. A comparatively new hobby, it naturally has the advantage of finds turning up more often than perhaps any other hobby. So while more speculative than postage stamps it has the excitement of finding something for a few pounds which may well be worth hundreds of pounds. There is a strong connection between stamps and banknotes in that often the engravers and printers are the same, and sometimes the same vignettes are used. Stamps were on occasion used as paper money and in contrast banknotes were overprinted and used as stamps.

So you see there is an affinity between both stamps and banknotes, which as both expand, will become more apparent.

STAMPS

THE PHILATELIC MARKET

Compared with an Ormolu clock, a Hepplewhite chair or a Picasso of the Blue period, a postage stamp may seem an insignificant item, but in the world-wide investment stakes it is far from being so. In fact, considering its size and content the postage stamp must rank as the most valuable single commodity in the world.

For instance, an unused Post Office Mauritius 2d Blue or 1d Orange-Red of 1847 works out at more than £40,000 for less than a square inch of paper! And those are just two of an ever increasing number of stamps whose value has now reached five figures.

People have been investing in stamps for many years, but it was not really until February 1973, when Stanley Gibbons, the world's oldest and largest stamp dealers opened an investment department, that stamp investment became accessible to the public at large. Since then, the belief of Gibbons' Board of Directors that Classic early postage stamps could compete favourably against nearly all other traditional forms of investment has been vindicated to the benefit and satisfaction of investors all over the world.

What, then, is the strength of the philatelic market? Will Classic stamps always be a good investment? And how should one go about forming a stamp investment portfolio?

One of the main strengths of the philatelic market is its international foundation. Stamp collectors are to be found the length and breadth of the globe, and stamp collecting is a hobby enjoyed by a complete cross-section of the population, from five-year-olds to kings, queens and presidents. It is almost certainly the most popular hobby there is, and philatelic clubs and societies abound in every town and country. Mr A L Michael, Chairman of Stanley Gibbons International Limited and one of the leading figures in world philately, maintains that stamp collecting is one of the most successful promoters of international friendship. This is confirmed by the number of highly successful national and international stamp exhibitions which are now held in most major countries. Some recent examples of these are: NAPEX (SOUTH AFRICA), PHILYMPIA (GREAT BRITAIN), STOCKHOLMIA (SWEDEN), INTERNABA (SWITZERLAND), BELGICA (BELGIUM), and ASDA (USA).

However, stamps do suffer from fluctuations in popularity, although this affects the value of Classic early stamps of the world less than later issues. Because of these, it is important that the would-be investor either gets to know his subject thoroughly or seeks the advice of experts like Stanley Gibbons. Gibbons will take all the hard work out of the investment for you if you haven't the time or inclination to take an interest in your stamps. They will advise you what to buy and when to sell; even find buyers for you and keep the stamps in their vaults, providing the investment is large enough to warrant this. But by far the most rewarding way to invest in stamps is to collect and take an interest in them yourself, thus deriving both pleasure and profit from the hobby.

To do this, it is necessary to select a country, island, period of history or area the stamps of which interest you and which offers scope for study and research. The stamps you choose to collect should also, obviously, fall within your price bracket. Of course, it is possible to put all your money into one or a few very rare and expensive items, lock them up in a bank vault and keep them until you wish to sell and take a profit. But this is costly and dull, tying up a large sum of money for many years. It is far more interesting, and far less expensive, to form a comprehensive collection of the stamps of your choice, thus spreading your investment and reducing the risk. Working on the formation of a fine stamp collection can be tremendously satisfying, quite apart from the financial aspect, and many well-known collections today have been formed over years of fascinating study which will pay off rich dividends when the time comes to sell. But more often than not superb collections of this sort do not come onto the market until the collector has died, because he becomes so attached to the stamps that he cannot bear to part with them. And even after he has died, his widow will often keep the stamps as a memento because he was so attached to them, (in many cases, despite the fact that she needs the money).

Philately offers an almost unparalleled choice of subject to the investor/collector. He can specialise in stamps on cover, early postal markings on cover, imperforate stamps, mail from wrecks, line-engraved or surface-printed issues, war correspondence, the mail of a particular postal area, high value stamps, imprimatur, artists drawings for stamps and many other categories.

The scope is unlimited and, if he finds he has gone as far as he can or wishes to go with a particular field of study, can sell and reinvest in something new. The aim is to create a saleable, attractive entity which is known in its field and has strength in its completeness. And for those who feel this might be too much to take on, there are partially complete collections on the market to which they can add without having to start at the beginning. These are often described in auction catalogues as suitable for further expansion and are nearly always a good buy. They exist for many reasons. Perhaps because a collector died, or maybe just because he wanted a change of subject. One recent example came up for auction at Stanley Gibbons described as follows in the auction catalogue:-

BRITISH HONDURAS

1789-1901, the collection, consisting of entires, stamps with original gum in singles and multiples as well as used on covers, attractively presented in album . . . .

Condition throughout is well above average and although reasonably complete this is in the basic stamps and there is much scope for expansion. The collection is already of major international award status and would ideally suit the collector seeking a new field of research and investment.

In forming a collection of stamps or postal history for pleasure and profit, membership of a philatelic club or society is helpful, if not essential. Almost every possible avenue of the hobby has a specialist club or society actively representing and promoting it. Attending and participating in the meetings and activities of one of these organisations can be very valuable in providing an exchange of knowledge and information; the opportunity to buy and swap items direct from collectors and keep abreast of the latest research and developments within the hobby; hear lectures and see displays by experts; and take part in local, national and international stamps exhibitions. Exhibiting your stamps can add to the value of the collection, particularly if awards are won. Today, more than ever before, the opportunities are available for the collector/investor to achieve this. Exhibiting under his own name, or a pseudonym, it is possible for his to become a named collection overnight, provided he has sought the right advice and studied and researched his subject thoroughly. He must also get to know how to present and write-up a collection, as this can mean the difference between winning and not winning an award at an exhibition.

An example of an item from named collections, showing the advantage of a pedigree for a comparatively low-priced item, is a portion of an envelope bearing 8d Bright Orange and 6d Grey stamps of 1855 of New South Wales. This item was sold in the Caspary auction in 1958 for £65, then passed into the collection of the famous philatelist and Swiss tobacco magnate, Maurice Burrus, which was sold in 1964, when the item fetched £110. It then became part of the outstanding collection formed by Lars Amundsen, a relative of the famous Norwegian Polar Explorer. And when Amundsen's British Commonwealth collection came up for auction at Gibbons in 1967, it made £250. Today, it is valued at £400 and listed as Ex. Caspary, Burrus and Amundsen.

Stanley Gibbons say that wise investment should be in Classic stamps issued pre-1900, especially the early imperforate issues. Their portfolios lie mainly within the £500 - £100,000 bracket, and are put together for the investor/collector as a medium to long-term investment over five or ten years. They emphasise that stamp investment is not for speculators, although in practice they have already found it necessary to go back to some investors to make an offer for portfolio items in a matter of months. Such is the demand for most of the big Classic rarities that substantial profits have, and can be, made in a very short time. The stamp market, like any other commodity market, is governed by the law of supply and demand, and at the Classic end of the market there are a rapidly growing number of collectors around the world trying to obtain a very limited number of fine stamps and other philatelic items. This situation has provided a few investors with the opportunity to make some excellent profits. For example, a city businessman who agreed to pay £20,000 for a used Post Office Mauritius was offered a profit of £5,000 on it before he had even paid for the stamp! Needless to say, he wisely turned down the offer and his investment is now worth £10,000 more than he paid for it. The same collector/investor paid £3,800 in 1968 for an example of the Edward VII 6d 'IR Official' of 1902-04 in mint condition, which realised £10,000 when he sold it again on October 27th, 1972. These are, however, the exceptions rather than the rule. Annual appreciations on 'Classic' portfolios generally lie within the fifteen to thirty per cent bracket.

The advantage of having your portfolio handled by a large concern like Stanley Gibbons is that they deal with both the collector and the investor and know exactly how the philatelic market stands at any given time. They keep a photographic record of all stamps in a portfolio and will advise, free of charge, when is the best time to buy or sell.

It is possible to invest so much per year or per month with them, and they will either choose the material for you, or offer you a choice of fine items purchased from collectors, dealers and auctions throughout the world. The cream of the world's finest collections passes through their hands and they can offer probably the finest selection of philatelic material in the world at any given time. Their unique position and reputation is the collector/investors' best security. In the past, when there has been speculation in a particular issue, such as occurred with Britain's World Cup 4d of 1966 overprinted 'England Winners' at the last minute, and the 1973 Isle of Man 15 pence Inauguration stamp in the island's first independent issue, Gibbons have maintained their selling and catalogue price and ignored 'flash in the pan' speculation. Rumours in the stock exchange, heavy buying of an island issue by continental dealers and large stamp exhibitions are some of the factors which have temporarily affected the popularity and price of stamps.

Whilst on the subject of speculation, a word of advice is also needed for those who may think, or be led to believe, that there is great value, and investment potential, in modern stamp errors. Very early errors are, in general, a sound investment and some of the world's most valuable stamps are among these. But modern stamp errors are becoming increasingly common — hardly an issue goes by without some major printing mistake being discovered — so the market is uncertain and some prices have fallen. If you really want to buy modern stamps for investment, perhaps the best issues are those for royal occasions such as the 1948 Royal Silver Wedding or the 1953 Coronation. The market is generally strong for these issues, especially complete mint sets including first day covers.

In general, modern philatelic material will not appreciate for many years to come, and the collector/investor should avoid following up schemes involving it, which have been successfully operated in recent years by a few disreputable stamp dealers. One of these dealers sold sheets of modern commemorative stamps to Investors at a high price, which they were later only able to sell back to the post office at considerably less than face value.

As already stated, stamps as an investment have many advantages over traditional forms of investment. They are easy to carry about and require the minimum of storage space. This fact was taken advantage of by Jewish Refugees from Germany at the beginning of the Second World War. Many of them put their money into stamps in which the German authorities at the border checkpoints took no interest and which they allowed them to take out of the country without question. Thus, thanks to postage stamps, many

Jewish people who might otherwise have salvaged nothing, were able to start a new life in another country. Another advantage postage stamps have at present over other investments is exemption from Capital Gains Tax provided no single stamp in a portfolio/collection sells for more than £1,000. This is another good reason for spreading your investment over a number of items rather than buying a few very expensive stamps, although many stamp investment experts say that the high rate of return gained from high priced rare stamps amply compensates for any tax liability. The number of 'Classic' rarities available outside museum and national collections is generally known and demand far exceeds supply. It is extremely unlikely that any substantial quantities of the early stamp rarities remain to be discovered, which gives the Investor the satisfaction of knowing exactly how many stamps of a particular issue are available, where they are and often the condition they are in. The market cannot therefore be flooded with a particular issue at any time and prices can only go in one direction — upwards. This gives rare stamps a distinct advantage over such commodities as diamonds or precious metals, which can be dug up in large quantities from the ground at any time, upsetting the delicate balance of the market and adversely affecting prices.

There is widespread fascination with very rare items, with 'the only one in existence' or 'one of only 20 examples known', and rare stamps offer the collector/investor the opportunity to indulge this whim. An excellent example of the demand and high prices fetched by rare 'Classic' stamps like this came on October 4th, 1973, when a Bermuda Penny 'Perot' on a lettersheet — one of only two examples known dated 1854, the other being in the Royal Collection at Buckingham Palace — reached a staggering £50,000, paid by an American collector. This Postmaster's Provisional stamp (illustrated on page 12) used on a lettersheet sent locally on April 16th, 1855 from Hamilton to St. Georges on the island, was first discovered in 1897 and bought by Philipp La Renotière Von Ferrary, the millionaire whose vast collection of rare stamps was taken by the French after the First World War and sold in Paris in the 1920s to pay off some of Germany's war debt. In the fifth session of this mammoth sale, in 1922, this Penny 'Perot' realised only 30,000 Francs which, with sale tax, was the equivalent of around £556. The next time it was sold in auction was in London at the Burrus sale on July 24th, 1963, when it realised only £11,000.

The history behind this stamp and other provisional issues of Bermuda is worth giving here to illustrate the top investment stamps of one area.

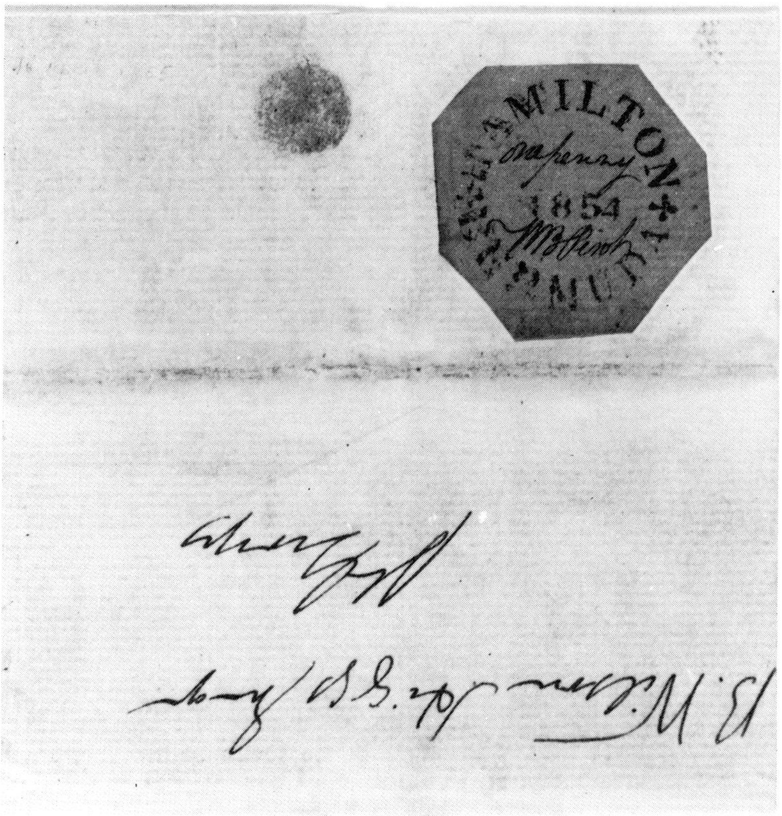

Like the Mauritius 2d and 1d rarities, the Bermuda 'Postmasters' owe their existence to one personality. In Mauritius it was a printer and engraver named Joseph Barnard and in Bermuda it was the Postmaster of the capital Hamilton, William B Perot. The circumstances of the issue are probably unique in the history of philately and make interesting reading.

From 1818 on the island the postmasters William B Perot, and Thomas Thies at St Georges, had been allowed to keep for themselves all revenue for inland mail. This system continued uninterrupted until 1842, when a new act reduced the inland postage rate to one penny per ounce for letters to be prepaid in all cases. Thus the Bermudan postal system was brought into line with Britain's and it became advantageous to the postmasters to promote the use of inland mail and ensure all letters were prepaid. But this was more difficult than might be imagined. People wishing to post letters would normally take them to the post office during the day and hand them over the counter with the correct postage money. The letters were then impressed with a datestamp and put in the mail bag. However, if a person was unable to get to the post office during opening hours, it was possible to post letters through the office door together with the correct amount for postage. Then the letters would be sent in the usual way when the office reopened.

More often than not, however, the Postmaster would find in the morning that there were more letters to post than there was money to pay for their postage. So he had to send some free of charge because it was impossible to tell who had put money in and who had not.

So Bermuda's postmasters lost considerable revenue and in Hamilton this situation occurred often enough to stir William Perot into doing something to try and stop it. He may have known of the Postmaster Provisionals introduced in the United States in 1845, or perhaps the idea was suggested to him, but anyway, he decided to produce special home-made postage stamps for the pre-payment of local letters and for use when the post office was closed.

The first stamps issued by Perot came out in 1848. They were made with the current datestamp, minus the month and the day of the month. These altered impressions he made many times on sheets of paper and then wrote in the value 'One Penny' (the standard rate for sending a local letter) above the year and put his signature beneath it. The stamps may also have been gummed on the back, as one example, thought to be unused, is certainly gummed.

Early "Postmasters" of 1848 and 1849 were impressed in black, but red ink was introduced in Hamilton during May 1849 and remained in use for sixteen years. The stamps were not known to collectors until 1897, when the specimen shown in the illustration above was found. The discovery of this great rarity of 1854 (only one other example exists of 1854) was followed by a second discovery in April 1898 when an example in black dated 1849 was bought by a collector.

This collector, a Mr B W Warhurst, wrote inquiring about the issue to the then Postmaster of Hamilton in June, 1898, who replied that he could not trace the stamps through official records, but from a 'reliable private source' had been able to confirm that they were used 'for prepaying postage within the Colony'.

Perot's first home-made stamps were in use at least until 1856. He remained Postmaster of Hamilton until 1862 and examples of a second type are known, the earliest of which is dated 1861. But it is not certain exactly when this new issue was introduced. 'Postmasters' were also issued at the Post Office at St. Georges on the island, but only a few examples dated between 1860-63 have been found.

The current catalogue listing for all these issues is as follows:-

1848-61. Postmasters' Stamps. Adhesives prepared and issued by the Postmasters at Hamilton and St. Georges.

(a) By W B Perot at Hamilton.
1 1d Black (1848,1849)............................ £ 9,000
" 1d Red/White (1853)............................ £10,000
" 1d Red/Blue (1854, 1856).................... £10,000
2 1d Red/Greyish Blue (1861)................ £ 4,000

(b) By J H Thies at St Georges. As type 2 above but inscribed 'St Georges'.

1d Red (1860).. £ 9,500

LEGENDARY RARITIES

No book on stamp investment would be complete without mention of the 1847 issues of Mauritius. Here is a comparison between the catalogue prices for these stamps in 1925 and 1974. A graph is included on page 18.

'Post Office' issues of 1847

1925	*Unused*	*Used*
1d Orange-Red	*£ 4,000*	*£ 2,500*
2d Blue	*£ 3,250*	*£ 3,000*
1974		
"	*£40,000*	*£27,000*
	£40,000	*£27,000*

Looking at these figures, it seems hardly surprising that these two stamps have become a legend far beyond the realms of the philatelic world. In fact, they have made the early stamps of Mauritius so famous that in Germany there is a philatelic magazine called 'Mauritius', in Japan there is a millionaire collector who specialises almost exclusively in the stamps of the island, and one collector even advertised for a wife to try and get an example of the 2d Blue for his collection. Here is his advertisement, which appeared in Vanity Fair in 1891, having been copied from a Mauritius newspaper:-

A Stamp Collector, the possessor of a collection of 12,544 stamps, wishes to marry a lady who is an ardent collector and the possessor of the blue two penny stamp of Mauritius issued in 1847.

Unfortunately history does not record whether he was successful, and today such romanticism has been replaced by the open cheque book.

Postage stamps were first issued in Mauritius — the first British Colony to have them — on September 21st, 1847, principally for use on invitations to a ball being held on the island by the Governor's wife, Lady Gomm. The two stamps, a 2d and 1d, were designed by Joseph Barnard, a miniature printer and engraver with poor eyesight, resident in Port Louis, who was, at the time, the only person in Mauritius with a practical knowledge of engraving.

Barnard charged £10 for engraving the plate and ten shillings per thousand for printing the 1d and 2d stamps. He was instructed to carry out the work some time in May 1847. The island's postmaster, J Stuart Brownrigg, gave him his brief one morning at the Post Office and the young man wandered away to do the work. However, after taking a few steps, it is said, some confusion arose in his mind over the instructions he had been given. What was it that he had to put down the left side of the stamp? He decided to return and ask the postmaster again, but on the way saw the words 'Post Office' in big letters over the Post-master's door. This seemed to jog his memory and he turned back towards his workbench. The result of this incident was that the words 'Post Office' appeared on the left hand side of the stamp instead of 'Post Paid'.

His design for the stamps was copied from Britain's Penny Black and engraved on a small copper plate 3¼" x 2½". As he was not a skilled engraver, his copy was crude, but has a charm which has certainly contributed to the stamps' popularity. One particularly interesting feature of the design is that the initials JB appear in tiny letters at the base of Queen Victoria's neck.

The stamps were printed one at a time. Five hundred of each issue were required, and, as can be imagined, the work progressed slowly. Barnard printed 350 of the issue and then reported to the postmaster. His error was discovered, but he was told to finish the work because the stamps were urgently needed for Lady Gomm's invitations.

When the stamps were eventually put on sale in September they were an immediate success. The entire issue was sold out in less than a week. But in fact the Mauritius Post Office made a loss on them. The cost of the engraving and printing was £10.10 shillings but the total face value of the 1,000 stamps was only £6.5 shillings.

Most of the 1,000 examples were either lost or destroyed, but a Madame Borchard, wife of a Bordeaux merchant, discovered a number among her husband's correspondence in 1867. She was a keen stamp collector, but her knowledge of stamps was limited. She had no reference to the stamps in her album and so swapped them with another collector. Since her discovery only fourteen other examples have been found, making in all twelve 2d's and fourteen 1d's known.

You may wonder what Madame Borchard received in exchange for her famous stamps? Well, she undoubtedly came away the loser because she took two Montivideo 'Suns', which today, unless they were the earliest and finest examples, would be worth less than £500 each.

Examples of the 1d Orange-Red and 2d Blue found their way into famous collections such as those of Baron Rothschild and Philipp La Renotière Von Ferrary. Around half the total number of copies known are now believed to be in museum collections and the rest are in private collections (the Royal Collection housed at Buckingham Palace contains examples of both stamps).

The fame of the 'Post Office' Mauritius issues has caused the second correct printing, and subsequent printings, of the stamps on the island to rise in value. The first of the 'Post Paid' printings was carried out in May 1848, using plates also engraved by Barnard. These were made of copper and had previously been used to print advertisements for the Grand Hotel d'Europe in Port Louis. They were put into service until they were worn out, and stamps showing many different states of the plates exist. Worn impressions can be bought for under £200 and are certainly a sound investment providing expert advice is sought before purchase, in case of any serious defects.

In Stanley Gibbons' October 4th, 1973 sale of British Empire 'Classics', two unused examples of the 1d 'Post Paid', earliest impressions, realised £5,000 each. And a 2d 'Post Paid', also of the first state, made £7,500. The latter, a corner copy with large margins,

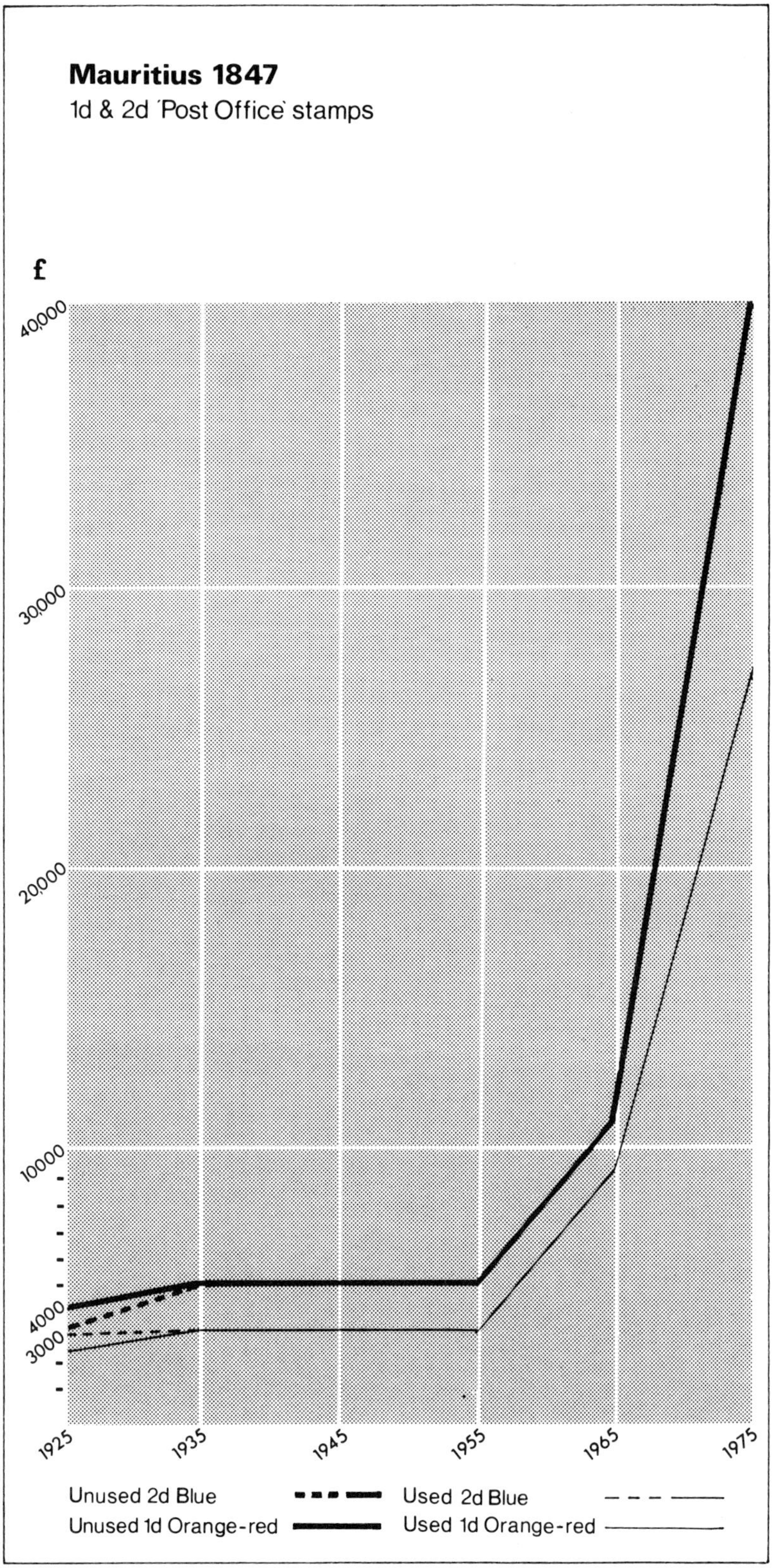
Mauritius 1847
1d & 2d 'Post Office' stamps
£
40,000
30,000
20,000
10,000
4000
3000
1925
1935
1945
1955
1965
1975
Unused 2d Blue
Used 2d Blue
Unused 1d Orange-red
Used 1d Orange-red

had previously fetched £1,300 in the first sale of the Ferrary collection in 1921. Early used examples of the 'Post Paid' also sold well for between £650 and £2,250.

A used example of the 2d Blue 'Post Office' Mauritius sold by Stanley Gibbons for £20,000 to a Collector early in 1973. The stamp is now estimated to be worth at least £30,000.

Choosing Stamps for a Portfolio

One accurate way of choosing stamps for your portfolio is to plot their progress in the past through reference to Stanley Gibbons' catalogues, the 'Stamp Collector's Bibles', which have been published continuously since 1865.

For example, the world's first postage stamp, the Penny Black of 1840, and its counterpart the Two Pence Blue, make interesting study:-

Great Britain

	1d Black of 1840		*2d Blue of 1840*	
	Unused	*Used*	*Unused*	*Used*
1865		*1d each*		*2d*
1895	*6/- (30p)*	*3d (1¼)*	*—*	*1/3d (6¼p)*
1905	*25/- (£1.25p)*	*6d (2½p)*	*£8*	*3/- (15p)*
1915	*25/-*	*2/- (10p)*	*£8*	*12/- (60p)*
1925	*60/- (£3)*	*5/- (25p)*	*£8*	*18/- (90p)*
1935	*85/- (£4.25p)*	*6/- (30p)*	*£18*	*15/- (75p)*
1945	*£12*	*20/- (£1)*	*£45*	*40/- (£2)*
1955	*£22*	*60/- (£3)*	*£80*	*£8*
1965	*£28*	*75/- (£3.75p)*	*£90*	*£16*
1974	*£150*	*£12*	*£300*	*£25*

For graphs showing the ever increasing value of these two stamps see pages 20 and 21.

Great Britain 1840

2d Blue

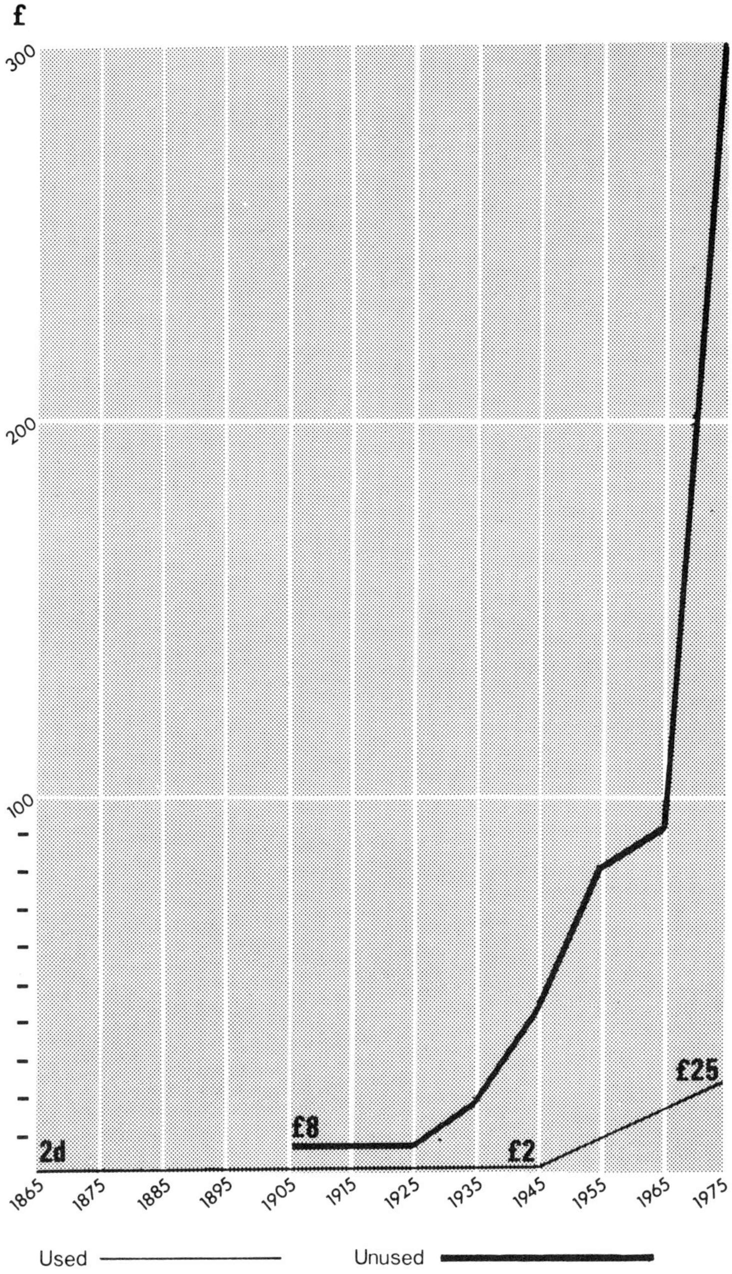

Great Britain 1840
1d Black

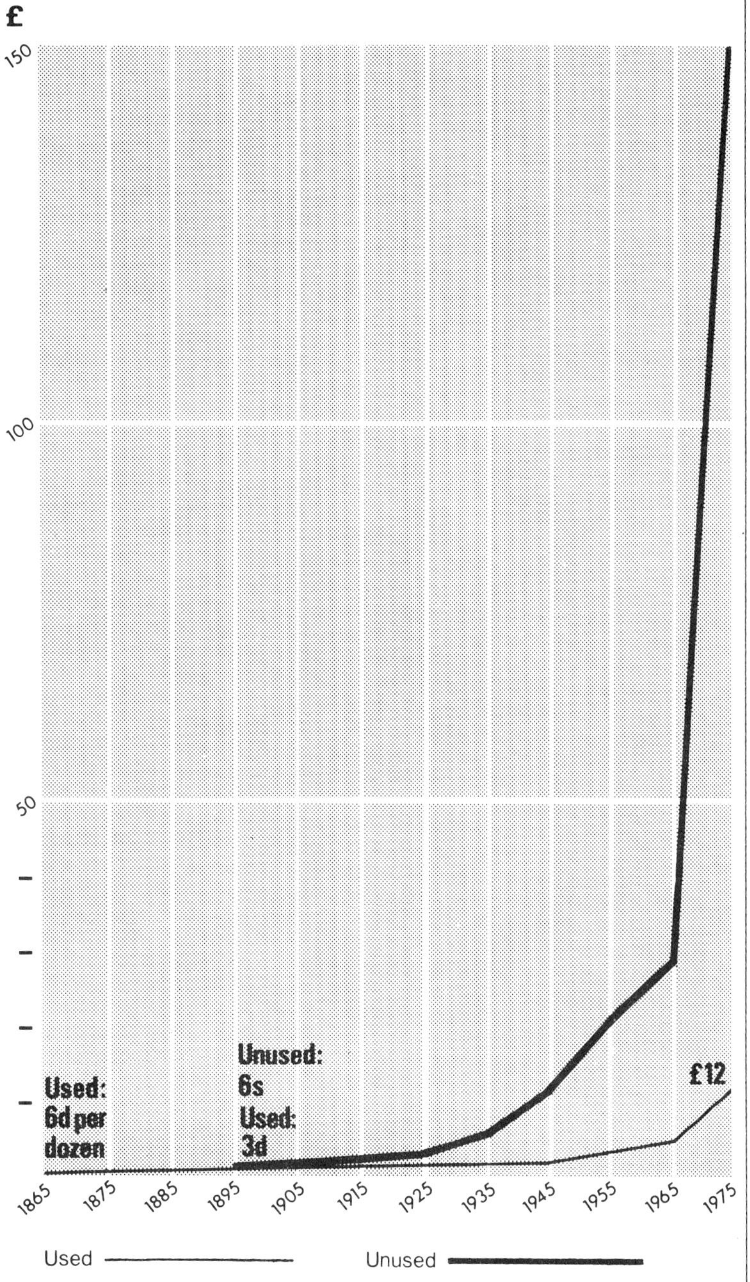

BLACKS AND BLUES

Prior to 1840 the postal system was complicated and expensive. The addressee usually paid for a letter on receipt not, as now, the sender. This led to many abuses and much paper work. For example, each letter was charged according to the number of sheets it contained and the distance it had to travel. A letter sent from London to Manchester might cost 11d; one to Glasgow 1/4d; and one to Ireland even more. The extra charge for an enclosure meant that each letter had to be held up to the light of a candle to see if it contained other sheets of paper. People found cunning ways of dodging the high postal rates and the famous promoter of the uniform Penny Post, Rowland Hill, once came across one of these when on a walking holiday in the Lake District. He saw a Postman call at a cottage door with a letter. A young woman answered and on being told the charge for the letter said she couldn't pay for it. Gallantly, Rowland Hill walked up to the house and offered to pay. Afterwards she told him he needn't have bothered. She knew the letter was from her fiance. He wrote every month and each time she refused the letter. The Postman's knock was enough to tell her that her fiance was well.

Another abuse was rife at the Houses of Parliament where Members of Parliament were allowed a free franking service for their mail. On one occasion an MP was observed to post 2,000 letters in a day for his own firm.

The spread of literacy meant more mail to be handled and a more costly and complicated service. Endless time was wasted by postmen checking the rates on letters and knocking on doors to collect postal charges. Yet Rowland Hill met untold resistance to his campaign for a Uniform Penny Post. He argued that it made sense to reduce the charges and introduce prepayment throughout, thus cutting down the administrative work involved, increasing the amount of mail, bringing in more revenue, and improving the postal service. And it did make sense. In 1838 the number of letters carried was 75,000,000. By 1841 this number had increased to 208,000,000. And by 1854 to 443,000,000.

But critics of the system were many. The Postmaster General at the time, Lord Lichfield, said that: 'With respect to the plan set forth by Mr Hill, of all the wild and visionary schemes which I have ever heard or read of, it is the most extravagant.'

Queen Victoria, however, backed Hill and said she was quite prepared to give up the Royal right to free franking for her mail in order to see the new service introduced. The Duke of Wellington was at first against the scheme, but reluctantly backed it in the end. Royal Assent was eventually given to the Uniform Penny Post scheme in August 1839.

By this time Rowland Hill had become a popular figure in the country and he was asked to supervise the operation of the scheme. The Treasury ran a competition offering a prize of £400 for the best design for covers and stamps, which resulted in 2,600 suggestions, but none of those submitted were considered good enough. However, these competition entries are also of interest to the collector and some remarkable designs are among them.

Eventually, it was decided to copy the head of the young Queen Victoria engraved on a medal by William Wyon to commemorate her visit to the City of London in 1837. This lovely head was chosen not so much out of patriotic zeal, but because it was thought that any flaw or difference in the Queen's profile would be instantly spotted.

Two stamps were produced by Perkins, Bacon and Petch. Printed in Fleet Street, they were the famous Penny Black and Two Pence Blue. The Penny was to pre-pay a half-ounce letter and the 2d to pre-pay a letter weighing more than half an ounce, but not exceeding an ounce. With painstaking care the portrait of the Queen was engraved for these stamps by Charles Heath and his son Frederick.

It is doubtful whether the work which went into producing these two stamps could be repeated today. The detail used to set in relief the head of the young Queen is exquisite, and each stamp was individually lettered to discourage forgery. They were produced in sheets of 240 and a total of eleven printing plates were used to print the 1d Black. Examples from some plates are more common than others. Plate 11, for example, was used to print only 700 sheets of 1d Blacks. For the 2d Blue of 1840, two printing plates were used.

Issued with the world's two first stamps in May, 1840, were the Mulready pre-paid covers. These had been originally considered as the main means of postage. But the Penny Black and Two Pence Blue were preferred by the public and the Mulready, which was designed to show the virtues of the postal service, was caricatured out of existence. Postage stamps won the day, although they were to run up against many more problems. Among these was a scare that licking stamps caused cholera!

Today, both the Penny Black and Two Pence Blue are to be found in collections throughout the world. An unused Penny Black in the 1975 Catalogue is listed at £175. In the last year it has increased by £50. Used, it has now reached a price of £14. These prices are for good average examples. Finer copies fetch much more, poorer examples, less.

A total of 68,158,080 Penny Blacks were printed, but it is impossible to say how many of these survive. Probably only a relatively small proportion. But what can be said with certainty is that the Two Pence Blue is much rarer. Only 6,462,960 Blues were printed and nowadays an unused example in an auction is something of an occasion. One which appeared in a Stanley Gibbons auction last June fetched £470 against an estimate of £250.

In Stanley Gibbons' first postage stamp catalogue of 1865 Penny Blacks were quoted at 6d (2½ new pence) a dozen and Two Pence Blues at 2d each. The 1975 catalogue listing for the 2d Blue is £450 unused and £35 used. Again, these prices are for good average examples.

When buying either a Penny Black or Two Pence Blue, look for one with four good margins. As they had to be cut from sheets of 240 by hand, Post Office Clerks were often careless. For this reason, a stamp from the beginning of the sheet often has better margins than one from the end. Also, multiples of either stamp are always a good buy, particularly blocks.

Both stamps are very attractive to collect on cover, especially if they have neat cancels and were posted in 1840. A good example of the Penny Black used on cover on the first day of issue, May 6th, 1840 is now worth around £1,000. Occasionally, examples are found posted on letters before the 6th. The earliest known of these is dated May 2nd. This is because the stamps were sent out to post offices around Britain before the 6th with instructions that they were not to be used until the official date of issue. But a few Postmasters seem to have ignored these instructions. Now these early letters have a special interest and value to collectors.

The printers were late in preparing and sending out the 2d Blue. Consequently no examples are known used on cover on the official date of issue, May 6th. The earliest known example on cover is dated May 9th. So clearly any 2d Blue of 1840 used on cover in May of that year is a considerable rarity and an excellent investment.

In February 1841, the colour of the Penny Black was changed to Red-Brown. In March of the same year the design of the 2d Blue was altered.

One fine investment item is this strip of twelve unused Penny Blacks which startled the philatelic world in June 1973 when it realised £6,500 in the same auction room where it had been knocked down for only £3,400 in November 1972.

Some investment ideas on foreign stamps

At the time of writing, Stanley Gibbons have been revising their catalogues for the stamps of countries outside Europe. So far they have covered countries from Abu Dhabi to Jordan and some considerable price increases are evident, illustrating how stamp values are going up worldwide.

The last time Gibbons undertook this mammoth publishing task was in 1970, when they produced their Parts II and III. Since then there have been increases of as much as 300% and more on single stamp prices. The new information contained in these catalogues should help investors to widen the scope of their collections and spread their investments over a number of countries.

A selection of stamps from the two volumes so far published follows. These have been chosen as representative of the many stamps included in these catalogues which show investment potential.

In Overseas 1 a tête-bêche pair of the Argentine Republic 15 centavos blue of 1862 (January 11th) has leapt from £3,000 for an unused pair and £2,000 for one used in 1970, to £12,000 unused and £6,500 used. Bolivia's 1866-68 5 centavos yellow-green is a lower priced stamp which has nearly doubled in price. In 1970 it was listed at £12 unused and £10 used. Now it is £20 used or unused.

Brazil's first stamps of August 1st, 1843, known as 'Bull's Eyes' because of their appearance, all show steady increases up to around 100%, and the continuing popularity of China's early candareen and candarin issues is reflected in marked price increases.

Overseas 2 includes what are perhaps the most remarkable price increases of all, among the early issues of Israel. Although this is a philatelically young country — its first stamps came out in 1948 — there has been much movement among all its issues, but particularly in prices for those early stamps with 'Tabs' (descriptive sheet margins attached to the stamps).

The complete set of nine unused stamps with 'tabs' which formed Israel's first issue of May 16th, 1948, has risen from £550 to £1,800 since the set was quoted in Gibbons' 1970 Part III catalogue. And the same sort of advance can be found at a lower level amongst individual stamps like the unused 20 prutot blue, with 'Tab', of March 31st, 1949, which has risen from £5 to £17 over the same period. The set of two stamps with 'Tabs' issued on April 23rd, 1950 — a 20 prutot chocolate and 40 prutot green — unused, has gone to £140 from £55.

Similarly high gains are evident among the now very popular stamps of Japan. The home market for all this country's issues is now strong, where not so long ago it was very poor. This has produced increases of as much as £2,000 on a single stamp price since the 1970 Part III.

The 20 sen red-violet of October 6th, 1872, for example, has risen to £2,500 for a used stamp from only £500. And the 30 sen grey-black of January-February 1874, has jumped up from £500 to £1,500 for an unused example, and from £100 to £600 for one used. The new price increases range across many issues, but are particularly evident among the early imperforate stamps.

The Dominican Republic's October 19th, 1865 1 reale black/yellow stamp on laid paper has risen from £200 unused and £160 used in 1970, to £300 and £250 respectively. And the medio reale olive on pelure paper of 1869, has reached £300 unused from £180.

Egypt's 5 piastres rose and 10 piastres slate of 1st January, 1866, in unused pairs (imperforate between), have gone up £50 each since 1970 and Guatemala's 5 centavos brown of 1871 in a tête-bêche pair (imperforate between) has risen from £75 to £500 unused.

Among comparatively cheap stamps, Haiti's 20 centimes red-brown/buff of 1881 has gone to £24 unused from only £8 in 1970.

Finally, among the issues of Iran (formerly Persia), the 8 shahis yellow-green of 1875 in a tête-bêche pair has risen a staggering £6,000 since 1970 to reach £6,500 used or unused.

POSTAL HISTORY

When investing in antiques of any sort, it can be helpful from the cost point of view to look ahead and try and guess in which direction collecting trends might go. If, for example, you could have foreseen the current vogue for collecting old photographs, cameras and camera equipment, you could have bought and sold at very advantageous prices. And the same applies to the work of some Victorian Picture Postcard Artists.

Looking into the future of stamp collecting it seems probable that more attention will be paid to postal history. This already growing off-shoot of stamp collecting is literally the study of the way letters travelled and the history of the posts.

The range of postal history material available at very reasonable prices is, at the moment, considerable, as a £13,500. Postal History auction held by Stanley Gibbons in London in March 1974 showed. This sale included a letter from Florence dated 1454, showing a superb manuscript Guild symbol, which realised £25, and a fine and rare letter from Naples dated 1459 showing Ferdinand of Aragon's personal embossed stamp — a crowned 'F' in a circle — which fetched £50. And if this last price seems reasonable for such a rarity, then it will seem even more so when you consider that embossed handstamps like this are probably the forerunners of all postal markings.

Another item you might be forgiven for thinking was worth hundreds of pounds, is a letter of 1657 written by a soldier serving with Cromwell's army at Neumegan during Britain's alliance with the French against Spain. It fetched just £40.

The forerunner of today's postage stamp was invented by Colonel Henry Bishop, who was granted the office of Postmaster General by Charles II in 1660 on condition that he paid the King £21,500 a year for the privilege. Before he had been long in this position, as often happened in those days, charges of misconduct were brought against Bishop who revealed in his own defence that: 'A stamp is invented that is putt upon every letter shewing the day of the moneth that every letter comes to the office, so that no Letter Carryer may dare detayne a letter from post to post; which before was usual'. Examples of Bishop's stamps or 'marks' on letters can, at the moment anyway, be bought for as little as £12.

Henry Bishop escaped his first inquisition, but when charges of delaying letters for up to ten days were brought against him in 1662, he was forced to give an account of his activities. This all proved too much for him and in April 1663 he resigned.

Bishop lived at Henfield in Sussex, where he was 'Buryed in Woolen only on 1692 Mar. 23', as a monument on the local church wall testifies. But his stamps lived on after him for another hundred years, and his idea was developed much further.

An example of an Exeter Bishop mark on a letter of 1706 sent to a recipient 'Att the Castle Taunton'.

This superb Bishop 'Mark' of April 9th, 1692, is used on an envelope letter sent from London to Edinburgh which realised £26 in Stanley Gibbons' Great Britain stamp auction in June 1974.

A fine example of a Dockwra 'PAYD PENY POST/PTV' marking used on an envelope letter sent from London to Chard in 1695.

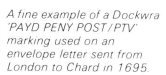

An early promoter of the uniform penny postage rate was William Dockwra, whose birth is given in the parish register of St Andrew Undershaft Church in the City of London as having been somewhere between 1616 and 1622. Between 1663-4 he was an Under Searcher in the Customs Office at the Port of London, then he turned his attention to the posts and 'for the benefit of the City [of London] and suburbs in point of charge and quick conveyance of Notes and Letters, ... projected a method of doing the same throughout for 1d a Letter'. Examples of letters carried by Dockwra's private postal service are known between December 1680 and November 1682, when the Duke of York, who had the monopoly of the posts, successfully brought an action against Dockwra for infringing his monopoly. Dockwra put up a brave fight for his 'Penny Post' and even petitioned the House of Commons. This petition, though unsuccessful in reinstating his postal service, which was taken over completely by the Government, gained him a compensation pension of £500 a year for seven years. Ironically, Dockwra was also made Controller of the Penny Post in March 1697, but it was found that: 'Mr. Dockwra is not fit to be entrusted in the office'.

Dockwra's pension expired in 1696, but it was renewed for a further three years. He applied for it again in 1700, but was this time refused. He died on September 25th, 1716, and his death was recorded in a journal of the day as follows:- 'Mr. Dockwra, frequently said to be the first Projector of the Penny Post, is dead, at near 100 years of Age.' Examples of letters carried by Dockwra's post can be bought for less than £100 at the moment.

Letters brought to the British Isles by ship in former centuries were marked at port of entry with a variety of different ship letter markings. Letters bearing any of these are usually scarce and there is a growing collectors market for them. Already prices are starting to rise. Two ship letter of particular interest shown on page 31, which were sold at Gibbons' March 1974 Postal History auction, are these of Glasgow and Lymington. The first realised £390 and the second £175, which, in view of their rarity, are very reasonable prices.

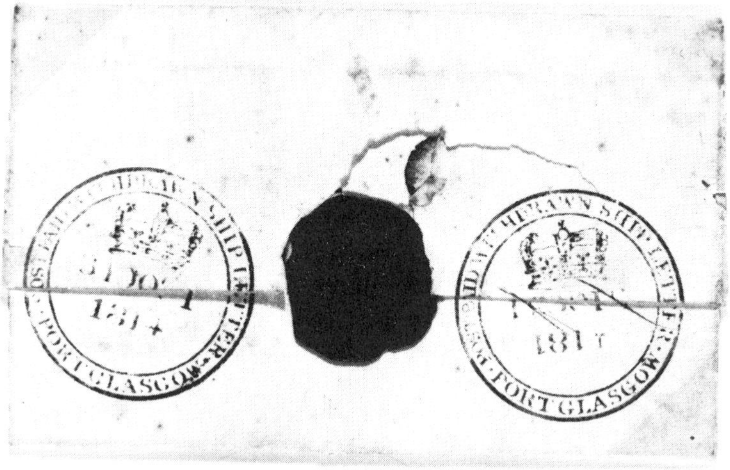

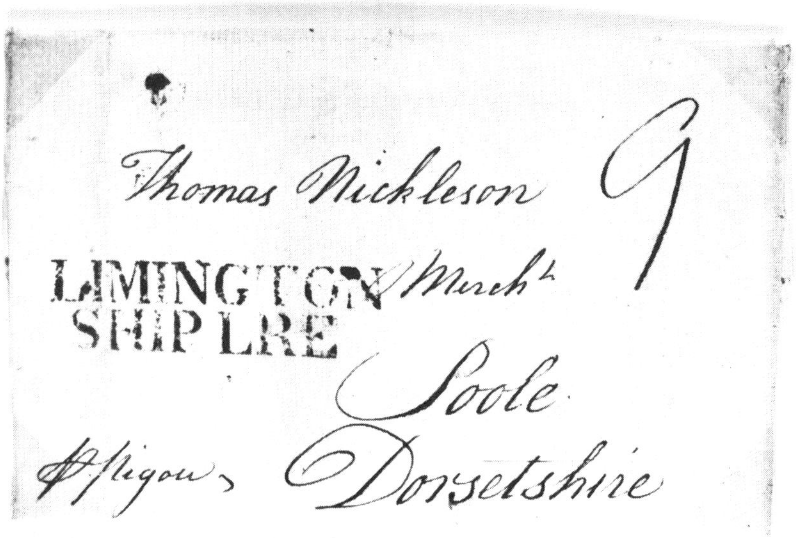

The Glasgow letter is addressed to Bordeaux and left Glasgow by ship for France on October 31st, 1814. On that day, the sender took the letter to the port postal receiving office where the Clerk applied a POST PAID. SHIP LETTER. PORT GLASGOW circular marking wrongly with the date upside down, so that he had to strike a second marking and cancel the first by hand with two pen strokes. This mistake alone makes the letter unique. But to add to its rarity and value, both markings are of a very scarce type only in use from September 17th, 1814, until July 11th, 1815. These two facts make the letter one of the most attractive and interesting early letters available to collectors.

At the time this letter was sent, there was a virtual war going on between the Postal Authorities and private shipping companies. Although an act of parliament had made it illegal for private vessels to carry letters — Post Office Packet ships being the only ones authorised to do so — the public continued to try to send their letters privately because it was cheaper. The revenue thus lost by the Post Office was considerable and in 1814, in an attempt to further discourage ship's owners from carrying letters privately, customs officials at all ports were given the power to search vessels and confiscate any letters found. However, the act which gave this power provided the following alternative:-

'The Post Master General shall receive letters directed to places, both within the King's dominions and kingdoms and countries beyond the seas, from persons who may be desirous to *forward them themselves*, upon payment of a third of the [post office] packet rates; and shall mark the postage and return the letters to the persons, who may forward them by *any vessels* not being packet boats, *without penalty*.'

The mark referred to was a special large circular handstamp, like the two used on the Glasgow letter, to be applied over the letter-join (see photograph on page 31) to prevent further insertions. This ingenious, though complicated scheme lasted only the ten months to July 11th, 1815. The special handstamp, which was only used on mail going overseas, is therefore very scarce, especially fine impressions of it.

The second item shown on page 31 is an attractive Limington (present day spelling : Lymington) ship letter marking of the type in use at the port's postal receiving office from 1777-1797. It was here used on a bulky letter brought from Pennsylvania 'Per (ship) Pigon' to Lymington for conveyance to a merchant in Poole in Dorset.

Today, Lymington is a little seaside town on the Hampshire coast which enjoys a considerable popularity with tourists and yachtsmen. But once, as this letter shows, it was a bustling maritime port of some significance. Salt was the mainstay of Lymington's flourishing trade and shipping commerce. But the development of the salt mines in Cheshire, and the return to prominence of Southampton as a port after a decline of two centuries, took away Lymington's importance as a port in the 18th Century.

During its heyday, Lymington, because of its sheltered position on the Solent and proximity to Portsmouth and other ports of call, was often used as a stopping off place by merchant sailing ships. And the pilots of these ships often brought letters ashore with them to post at Lymington. In addition to this mail, ship letters posted at Yarmouth were brought across the 3½ mile channel to Lymington by ferry for transmission.

The marking on the letter shown in the illustration is the first recorded for the port, although earlier markings may have been used. Early ship mail surviving from this attractive port is very limited because of its brief period of importance. On arrival at the port, early ship letters were also marked in pen with the postal charge. The letter shown here, because of its unusual bulk, was charged ninepence, of which 1d or perhaps 2d went to the Captain of the *Pigon* which had brought it to Lymington.

The postal history material so far mentioned in this section is just some of the fascinating and comparatively inexpensive material at present available to the investor/collector which, if demand continues to expand, would provide an excellent return in years to come for a modest outlay made now.

Other fields of postal history include mail showing the various mileage marks that were used on the old post routes, and letters from prisoner-of-war camps, battlefields and shipwrecks, to name just a few.

An interesting example of wreck mail is this letter (see illustration below) recovered from the wreck of the ship *Mexican* sunk off South Africa's Table Bay on April 5, 1900 after colliding in fog with the troopship *Winkfield*, bringing Imperial Yeomanry soldiers and remounts to the Boer War.

The *Mexican's* entire crew of 137 and 100 passengers, were taken to safety aboard the *Winkfield* on the evening of April 4th, 1900, but no attempt was made to salvage mail until the following morning, shortly before the *Mexican* finally sank. A correspondent of the Times who was at the scene reported that: 'As many of the mail bags as could be saved were brought off the *Mexican.*'

Covers marked RECOVERED FROM WRECK OF MEXICAN, in red ink, are rare.

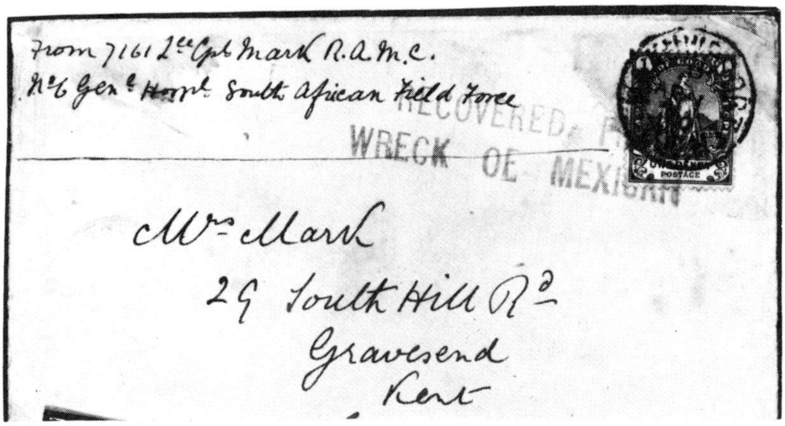

STAMPS AROUND THE WORLD

Although early stamps of Great Britain are among the most soundly backed from the marketability point of view, early stamps of almost all countries with an established philatelic history offer considerable scope for the investor among the lower priced 'Classics'; quite apart from the obvious attraction of such expensive rarities as the Hawaiian 'Missionary' 2 cents Blue at £30,000 unused, the British Guiana 1 cent Black on Magenta of 1856, the world's most valuable stamp now catalogued at £130,000 (although it was insured for £200,000 at a London stamp exhibition in 1965), and Canada's 12d Black of either 1851 or 1852-57 at more than £10,000 each.

The world's most valuable stamp at £130,000. Only one example is known.

One item of the many worthy of attention is Ceylon's 1857 4d Dull Rose, for which see the graph shown on page 49.

Swastika Overprinted Stamps increase by nearly 200%

British stamps overprinted with a Swastika by the Germans for use in the Channel Islands during the Second World War occupation, have shown an increase of nearly 200% since March 1973 according to the latest edition of Stanley Gibbons' full colour publication 'Collect Channel Islands Stamps' published in August 1974. In the previous edition the overprints, which were prepared for use but never issued because of the strength of local feeling against them, were quoted at £35 each. Now they have shot up to £100 per stamp.

The early postmarks of the islands on cover have also risen steeply. For example, Alderney's black Maltese Cross cancellation used for franking the island's mail between 1843 and 1845 has risen from £300 to a listing of 'from £1,200' (see graph on page 48). Even the tiny island of Herm has been affected by the almost unprecedented demand for Channel Islands stamps and postal history. Its double-circled datestamp in black of 1925-38 has gone up from £35 to £50. This was the only handstamp used on Herm prior to the Second World War.

Among pre-stamp markings on cover which have risen are Jersey's black marking of 1794-9, which has gone from £75 per example to £90 since the last edition. Guernsey's scroll type marking of 1807-10 has reached £80 from £65. And Jersey's ship letter markings of 1837 (in Red) and 1851 (in Blue), have both risen by £100 over the last sixteen months. The first, from £200 to £300, and the second from £300 to £400. Similar increases can be seen for two of Guernsey's ship letter markings on cover. The black 'Oval' marking of 1802-15 has gone from £200 to £300, and the 1836 'Boxed' type India Letter marking from £300 to £400.

The Great Stamp Forgery

One of the most attractive stamps to collect must surely be the Stock Exchange One Shilling Green forgery. For those who want not only an attractive stamp, but a talking point, this stamp is visual proof that the old adage 'Crime doesn't pay' has a shaky foundation.

This daring fraud is still largely a mystery today. The story begins with the transfer of lines from the old Telegraph Companies to the Post Office in January 1870. As with postage, a uniform rate was then fixed for private messages of one shilling for twenty words, whereas before rates had varied according to the distance over which the message was to be sent.

This uniform change led to an increase in the number

of telegrams from 8,606,000 messages in the first year under the post office to 17,346,000 in 1873.

Because of the transfer, the post office had to take on more staff and it was probably at this time that the man (or men) responsible for the forgeries was employed.

The charge for sending a telegram was prepaid with postage stamps, either a one shilling green or other stamps in combination, stuck to telegraph forms. Usually, clerks at the post office stuck on these stamps for customers and this practice continued until the forgeries were discovered.

The general increase in the telegraph business was particularly marked at the Stock Exchange Post Office in the city and it was there that the forgeries were used. Thousands of messages were sent out daily from this office informing people of what had been bought and sold at the stock exchange. The completed forms were passed through a grille to the Clerks who would then stick on the shilling stamps before the message could be sent. This gave the Clerk (or Clerks) with forged stamps the perfect opportunity to substitute them for the real thing and put the money in his pocket.

Thousands of these stamps were used somewhere between June 1872 and June 1873, though it is possible they were used both before and after these dates. It has been estimated that more than £30,000 was made out of these forged stamps, but the only evidence is the number of examples that were eventually found.

The person or persons responsible for this fraud wisely stopped using the stamps when they had made a good sum and the crime remained undetected until 1898, when Charles Nissen, the famous philatelist, found one shilling green stamps with no watermark and impossible lettering amongst a quantity of telegraph forms stolen by workmen from a pulping mill in Essex.

Charles Nissen realised he had found something important and with the help of other philatelists bought up more forms from the mill. They found forged stamps used either singly or in combination with real stamps. But never more than one forged stamp on any form. The faulty stamps also show colour variations and other minor differences.

A Post Office inquiry was set up to investigate the fraud, but little is known about what was discovered. The file on the subject is not complete although it has been said in print that one culprit was caught. But as he was then an old man, having retired early, no charges were brought.

It is possible that the full history of the forged shilling green will always be a mystery. In fact, there are still two schools of thought as to how they were produced. Some say one at a time, others in blocks.

Seven examples can be seen in the Phillips' collection at the National Postal Museum and some are contained in the Gibbons' reference collection. One with possible lettering can be bought for £45 and one with impossible lettering for £50, though this price can vary according to condition and date used. An example recently fetched £50 at auction, but a stamp from the rare Plate 6 would realise much more. A few years ago the forgeries were selling at £30 each. As an investment, the stamp gives prestige and interest to any collection.

The Stock Exchange One Shilling Green forgery (right) used in combination with genuine stamps.

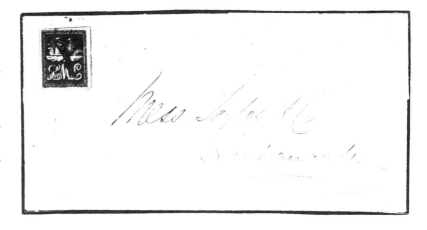

This is an example of the famous 5 cents Blue stamp issued in April 1847 by David Bryce, owner of the SS Lady McLeod *for the pre-payment of the carriage of letters sent on his ship which sailed between Port of Spain and San Fernando. In the Charlton-Henry auction in New York in December 1961, this cover fetched £700. In 1973, at an auction in London, it realised £3,000.*

An attractive cover addressed to New York, bearing Nova Scotia's 1851-57 1d red-brown, 3d deep blue and 6d yellow-green to make up a 10d double rate from Halifax.
The item travelled to New York by packet boat. Fewer than ten examples of this ten penny rate on cover for Nova Scotia are thought to exist.
In the Dale-Lichtenstein sale in America on November 21st, 1968, the cover shown here was sold for $6,500, the equivalent of around £3,000. In 1973 at a London auction it fetched £4,000.

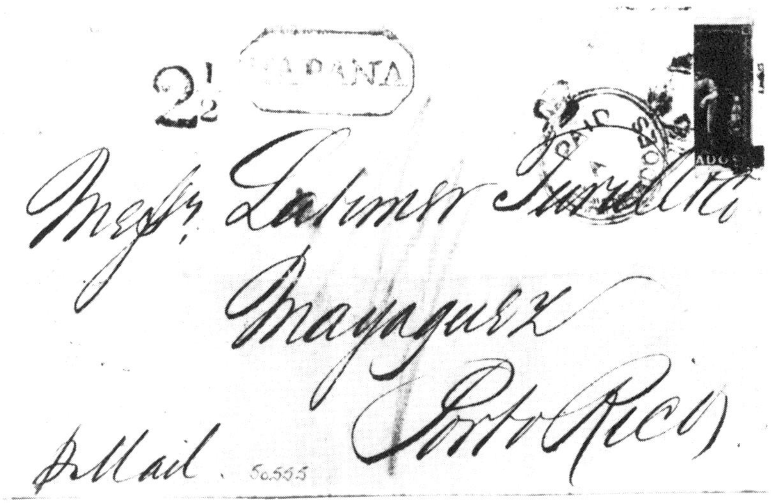

This attractive cover addressed to Porto Rico and bearing a Barbados 2d greyish-slate stamp of 1852-55 bisected to serve as a 1d stamp, realised £290 in the Amundsen British Empire sale on December 6th, 1967. In 1973 it fetched £950 at auction.

Canada's famous 12d Black of 1851 (unused) on laid paper. This example was sold in the Dale-Lichtenstein auction in New York on November 18th, 1968, for £7,100. Described as a blue-chip investment of the first order, it has not been sold at auction since, but is valued by experts to be worth in excess of £16,000 at the time of writing.

Used strip of four of British Guiana's 1852 1 cent black on magenta on an entire letter written at "Plantation Spartar" on March 1st, 1855, and sent to George-town.
In the Burrus sale in London on November 26th, 1963, this item fetched £6,000. In 1973 at Stanley Gibbons' 'Classics of the British Empire' sale it made £12,500.

Horizontal pair of British Guiana's 1850 'Cottonreel' (so called because of its shape and appearance) 12 cents blue. It was sold in the Ferrary Sale in Paris on June 23rd, 1921, when it realised £264. In 1973 Stanley Gibbons sold the same item at auction for £2,500.

Ceylon's 8d brown of 1859 in unused condition. This stamp was sold in the Da Silva auction in London on January 12th, 1959, for £420. Again in the Amundsen sale, also in London, on December 6th, 1967, for £1,100, and most recently in 1973 for £1,900.

An exceptional and very rare tete-beche block of four of Finland's 5 kopecks issue 1856.
The block has one of the finest philatelic pedigrees, having passed through the Ferrary, Faberge, Caspary, Lichtenstein and Amundsen collections. When the Lichtenstein collection was sold in America in December, 1966, it made the equivalent of around £6,000. It was last sold at auction by Stanley Gibbons when they offered the Amundsen collection of Finland and Switzerland for sale in London on November 2nd, 1972. It then fetched £12,500.

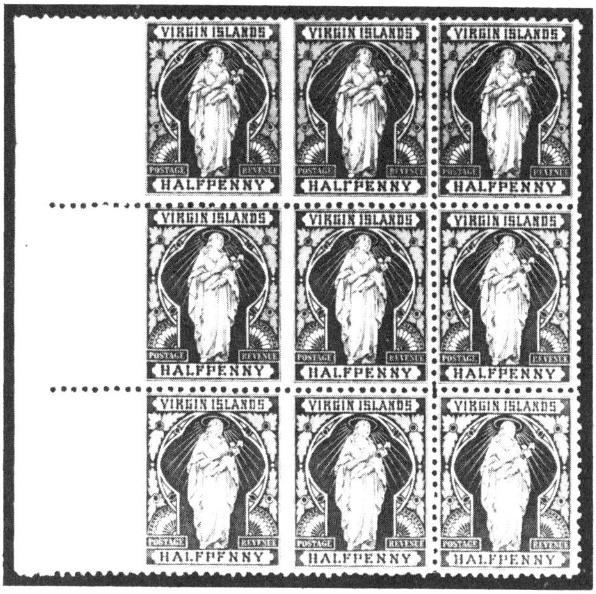

A marginal block of nine of the Virgin Islands 1899 ½d yellow-green containing not only two errors in the spelling of halfpenny, but also three horizontal pairs imperforate between. This interesting and rare item was sold in the Charlton-Henry sale in New York on April 7th, 1961, for just under £400. In Stanley Gibbons October 4th, 1973, sale it fetched £1,900.

Britain's rarest normal postage stamp, the famous Edward VII 'IR Official' 6d. Dull Purple of 1904. The stamp is rare because it was issued shortly before all overprinted stamps used by Government departments were withdrawn from use.
An example sold at auction by Stanley Gibbons on October 27th, 1972, fetched £10,000. It was offered for sale on behalf of a wealthy businessman and collector,.The stamp is now catalogued at £13,500, which represents an increase of £8,000 in a little over three years.

An example of the famous 'Double Geneva' issue of 1843 cut vertically instead of horizontally. Less than five such pairs are known. This particular, used, vertical pair showing two neat red 'rosettes' cancellations was sold on November 2nd, 1972 by Stanley Gibbons in the Amundsen Finland and Switzerland sale for £22,000. It is now thought to be worth £32,500.

Rhodesia's £1 scarlet and reddish mauve error of colour of the 1910-16 issue. In 1973 this stamp was sold for £1,500. As it is a corner copy with margins, it is a particularly desirable example of the error and will appreciate rapidly. In 1964 the error was catalogued at £80 and in 1968 at £300.

This is a superb marginal example of Gibraltar's most famous stamp, the 1889 10 centimos 'Value Omitted' error which was sold at auction in London on November 23rd, 1973, for £1,400. In 1964 the error was catalogued at only £375 unused.
Only a few copies are known. They were printed in error without the value and somehow passed the checkers at Messrs. De La Rue and Company. It is recorded that a Colonel Arthur Egerton, DSO, who was stationed in Gibraltar in 1896, claimed to have bought two copies, one for £2 and another for 15 shillings. Examples of the error were also discovered and bought by the then Head Clerk at the Gibraltar Post Office, who later resold them at a high price.

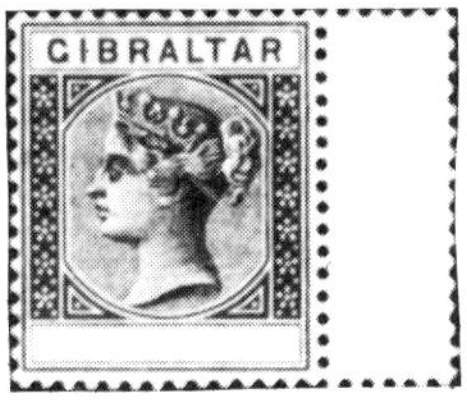

This attractive item is contained in the collection of Dr Douglas Latto, the well-known Harley Street gynaecologist and distinguished philatelist. It is a superb example of the first postage stamp, Britain's Penny Black, from the first position on the sheet of 240 stamps (corner letters A — A) and used on cover on the first day of stamp issue, May 6th, 1840. Five years ago a cover like this was worth only £250. Today they fetch over £1,000 each.

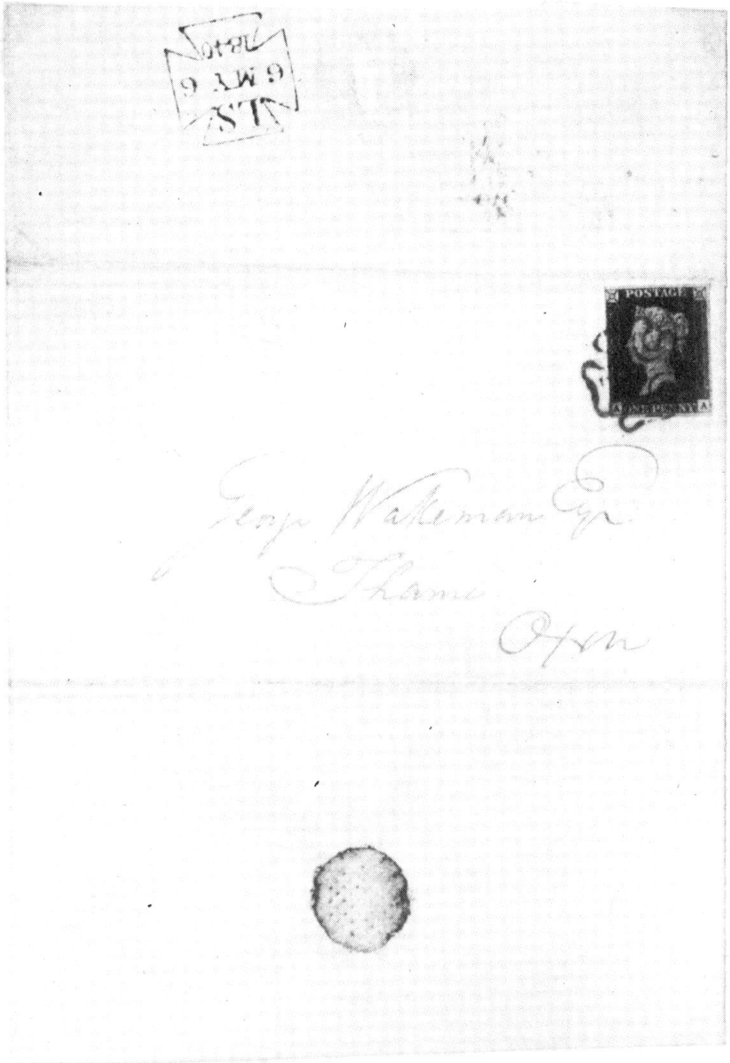

An unused example of Ceylon's 9d Purple-Brown of 1859. This beautiful stamp was sold in the auction of Baron De Worms collection in London on June 20th, 1938, for £420. Again in the De Silva auction on January 12th, 1959, for £875, and in the Amundsen auction, held by Gibbons on December 6th, 1967, for £2,200. In 1973 Gibbons sold it at auction again in London, when it fetched £3,000.

An attractive used block of four of the Van Dieman's Land (Tasmania) 1d carmine issue of 1855. In the Caspary sale in New York in 1958, this block fetched the equivalent of about £55. In Stanley Gibbons' 'Classics' sale on October 4th, 1973, it fetched £750.

The Virgin Islands famous 'Missing Virgin' error on the 1867-70 1 shilling rose-carmine issue. Around six examples of this error are thought to exist. It is very seldom seen on the market, but this example was sold at auction in London in 1973 for £13,000. It had been estimated to fetch only £8,000.

A superb unused corner block of four of the New South Wales 6d vermilion and prussian blue of 1859. This block fetched £82.50p in the Snowden Sale in London in 1944. It was not sold again at auction until Gibbons' Classics sale on October 4th, 1973, when it realised £550.

Thousands of pounds on stamp values

Rare stamps of many European countries have shown increases in price of 100% and more in the last twelve months according to Stanley Gibbons Europe 1 Foreign Postage Stamp Catalogue, published in August 1974.

The new volume lists and prices the stamps of all European countries from A to F and shows some extensive repricing in accordance with the current demand for all fine stamps.

At the top end of the market, the demand for 'Classic' early issues continues to push prices higher and higher.

Finland's 5 kopecks blue of 1858 on laid paper has risen from £5,000 to £9,000, and the very rare tête-bêche pairs of France's 1 franc orange of 1849-52 have reached listings of £35,000 unused and £22,000 used from £25,000 and £15,000 respectively.

France's 1 franc orange-vermilion of 1849, unused, has reached a listing of £5,500 per stamp from £3,500, and the 10 centimes bistre-brown of 1852, also unused, has risen by £1,000 to £3,000.

A more modern issue of France which has risen noticeably is the 50 franc ultramarine stamp of 1936 showing 'An Aeroplane Over Paris'. This stamp has gone from £65 to £100 unused, and from £35 to £55 used.

Belgium's first stamps of 1849, known as the 'Epaulettes', show marked increases. The 10 centimes brown has risen from £300 to £400 unused, and from £9 to £15 used. And the 20 centimes greenish-blue has gone to £550 from £400 unused, and to £14 from £10 used.

The very popular and attractive set of twelve stamps issued by Belgium in 1933 for the 'Orval Abbey Restoration Fund' has increased from £110 to £200 unused, and from £100 to £190 used. The set of seven 'Anti-Tuberculosis Fund' stamps issued the previous year, has also risen significantly, reaching £28 from £13 unused, and £24 from £9 used.

Demand for Austrian stamps

Considerable movement is also evident among Austria's ever-popular 'Classic' issues. The 2 kreuzer black of 1850, for example, has reached £250 from £120 unused and £12 from £6 used. And the 6 kreuzer brown in the same issue has gone to £150 from £70 unused, and to £90 from £35 used.

Even the stamps of traditionally less popular countries and periods have gained significantly. The set of nine overprinted commemorative stamps issued in 1930 during the Italian Occupation of the Aegean Islands has gone to £100 from £65 unused, and to £40 from £23 used.

Among the Balkan War issues for the Greek Islands, the 25 lepta ultramarine stamp of 1913 for the island of Khios with the Greek overprint inverted has gone from £7 used or unused to £15.

Albania's 10 paras green of 1913, unused, has increased from £8 to £18, and from £7 to £16 used. The same stamp with the overprint inverted is now listed at £50 used from £25. The 1 piastre ultramarine from the same issue has doubled from £3 unused to £6, and from £2 to £4 used.

Two further volumes for Europe covering the countries from G to P and Q to Z have just been published. Many other similarly good investment items are to be found in these catalogues.

The Much Mocked Mulready

Issued with the world's first adhesive postage stamps, the 1d Black and 2d Blue, in May, 1840, were the now famous Mulready 1d and 2d envelopes and wrappers. These were designed by William Mulready, R.A, and it appears that Sir Roland Hill expected a far greater demand for them than for the adhesive stamp.

But the British public preferred the postage stamp. And for reasons which are hard to understand today, found the design of the Mulready hilariously funny — so much so and so quickly that within one week after the first day of issue Rowland Hill was writing: 'I fear we shall be obliged to substitute some other stamp for that designed by Mulready, which is abused and ridiculed on all sides.' (It is interesting to note that the term 'stamp' had not at that time become restricted almost entirely to adhesive postage stamps, as it is now).

In fact, the design of the Mulready gave rise to a spate of caricature envelopes and much lampooning in the press of the day.

After a life of only months, the Mulready cover was finally withdrawn in 1841 and a large remainder in bulk stock destroyed.

Today, both the Mulreadys and caricatures of them are much sought after by collectors. At the time of writing the Mulready illustrated below, which was posted on the first day of issue, May 6th, 1840, from London to Sussex, realised £260 in a recent Stanley Gibbons auction. It is cancelled with a red Maltese Cross in the statutory position over the figure of Britannia.

Alderney 1841

Maltese Cross
cancellation on cover

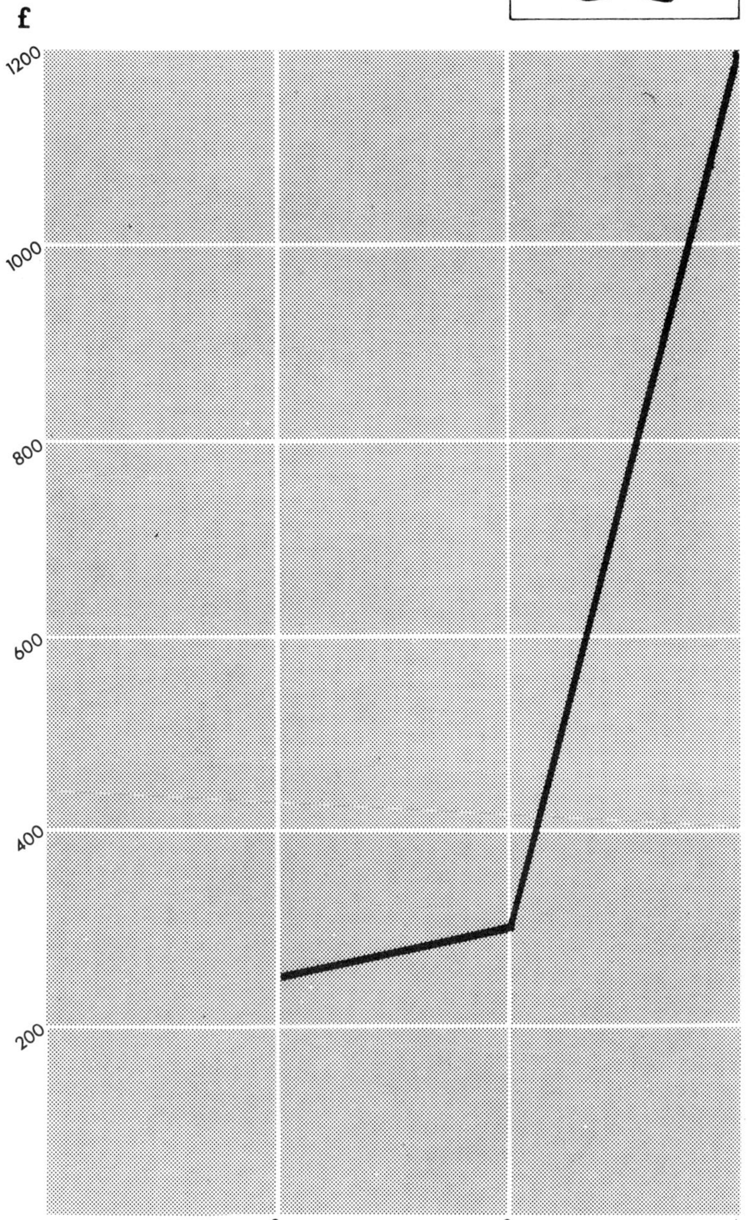

Ceylon 1857
4d Dull Rose

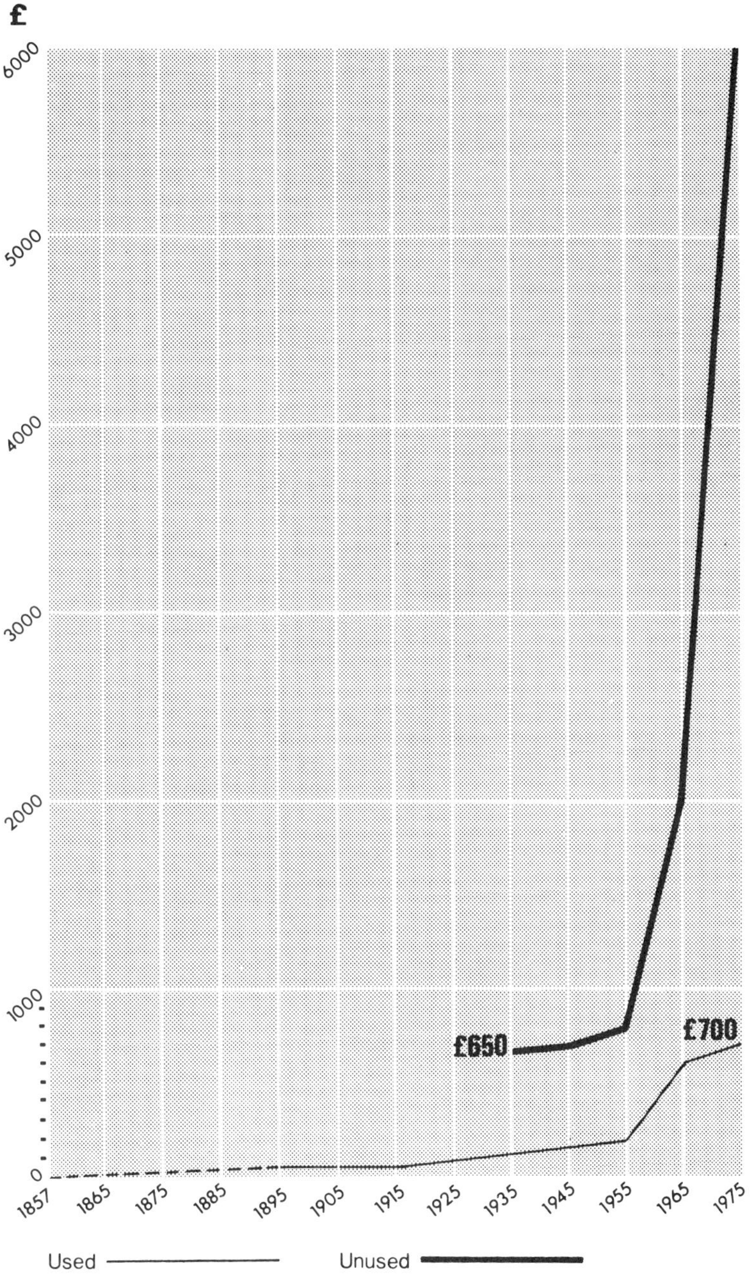

STAMPS AS MONEY

Fish hooks, bricks of tea, playing cards and slave girls all have one thing in common with postage stamps — they have all been used as money at one time or another. But while slave girls are a bit difficult to collect today, there is a growing collector interest in stamps used as money.

Values are rising rapidly because there is a strong market for them among stamp collectors. Also, Notaphily (see Section 2 of this book) is quickly developing into a major hobby and notaphilists are buying up these money-stamps as soon as they come on the market.

Using stamps as money began during the American Civil War. America's national debt was 76 million dollars and at the suspension of specie payment on the outbreak of war in 1862, postage stamps began to circulate as currency. Both the South and North had begun hoarding gold and silver, which created a shortage of small change that led, inevitably, to their use.

An astute American, John Gault, saw that stamps soon became dirty and torn, so he invented a special mica-fronted disc to preserve them. His 'Postage Stamp Case' was granted a patent on August 12th, 1862, and was soon in demand. Gault also sold the space on the back of the discs for advertising.

Finally, however, the US Government refused to supply any more stamps to Gault because the Post Offices even in the large cities were running out of stamps and it was clear Gault's operation was being run on a huge scale. The American Treasury came to the rescue of the public and replaced the discs with postage currency — small notes with designs of postage stamps on them, representing the value of the note. The first issue was even perforated like stamps. But before long this currency was itself replaced by fractional notes.

By the time all this happened Gault, once a Boston sewing machine salesman, was well on his way to becoming a millionaire and a total of 188 varieties of encased American postage stamps are known today.

During the Boer War the Civil Commissioners of Bulawayo mounted stamps on cards with an inscription saying: 'Please pay in cash to the person producing this card the face value of the stamp affixed thereto, if presented on or after August 1st, 1900'. The cards were signed by H Marshall Hole and many varieties exist. In fact, around £20,000 worth of this stamp currency was issued.

The Russians developed the idea further. In 1915 they simply printed sheets of stamps on card paper and had the backs printed: 'On a par with silver'. The stamps could then be used either as money or for posting letters.

When the Spanish Civil War was in progress, a spate of stamps were issued stuck to circular cards about the size of a crown piece. These were soon followed by emergency issues of stamp-money in Denmark, France and Italy.

Very little is known about many of the stamp-money issues and there is much for the collector to research.

One little known issue appeared during the 1914-18 war and just after when all silver coins disappeared in Germany — not only hoarded by private citizens, but also by some of the larger municipal councils. This led to a situation where it was impossible for tram conductors to give change, so stamps were attached to special cards produced by the tram firms and given in change. And in 1919-20 another obscure issue was made using Austrian stamps reprinted on grey cardboard and used as paper money.

Money-stamps issued during the inflationary period in Germany were readily accepted as change and even the larger hotels began to give them as small change. Items from this period are very rare and costly.

In the Ukraine at about the same time, they were short

of paper. So to overcome this, sheets of banknotes which had only been printed on one side, were used for printing stamps.

The exact reverse was the situation in England in 1914 when war was declared on Germany. The Treasury rushed out 10 shilling and £1 notes expecting, rightly, that gold would be hoarded. Paper supplies were low and sheets of stamp watermarked paper were appropriated for banknote printing.

Stamps have another use for banknotes as well — that of changing their value. Special 'tax' stamps have been printed by many countries, notably Czechoslovakia, Germany and Yugoslavia, to be affixed to banknotes when revaluing them.

Postage stamps circulated as money in many parts of the world during the Second World War when coins were in short supply. Although most of this was unofficial it was certainly recognised in Cyprus, where certain stamp values were 'unofficially' allowed to serve as currency, even in Government departments.

Examples of money-stamps from Spain, Denmark, France and Russia

Two examples of John Gault's now valuable and sought after money-stamps. 188 varieties of American postage-stamp money are known to exist. They turned John Gault from a Boston Sewing Machine Salesman into a millionaire.

This general acceptance of stamps as money led many towns and villages to issue token card money in the size of stamps and even perforated like stamps.

The prices of money-stamps vary considerably. Stanley Gibbons' current prices are: Gault money-stamps £30-£400; Boer War £30 each; French £4 each; Danish £7 each; Spanish Civil War £1 each; Ukraine 50 pence each and Russian 25 pence each (£9 a sheet).

As an investment, money-stamps offer two essential ingredients: rarity and growing demand. From a few pounds three years ago, Gault money-stamps have shot up in price and are likely to continue to rise in value. But there is obvious scope for investment even in the lower priced items, as the market is expanding on a world-wide basis.

POSTSCRIPTS

Europe, Asia and the Americas
by A Semel, Stanley Gibbons Limited, specialist buyer for European and Overseas Stamps

Naturally enough there is no great homogeneity in the stamps of European and overseas countries. When, however, someone wants to put together a portfolio of stamps it is advisable for him to concentrate on one or two countries rather than form a portfolio without any design. In Europe the nearest approach to this might be the first Common Market countries, excluding Italy, a country which at the moment is not interesting from the investment point of view. At the same time it is best to concentrate on the 'classics' or on the 19th Century of the countries concerned. This article will therefore examine the stamps of some countries and try to give the would-be investor indications for possible portfolios in this area.

Holland has had a surprising rate of increase in the prices of its stamps. Some of the basic stamps are of relatively low catalogue value, but on the open market their values have shown some surprises, and in some cases been outstanding in their increases. Both the stamps of Holland and Belgium have been popular and customers have been encouraged by dealers to go in for these countries, thereby creating a demand which has had the natural result of increasing prices.

At one time the first issues of Holland were comparatively easy to find, however the specialist demand has to a great extent altered this. The demand has been affected by the research that has gone into the stamps, culminating in the fact that these stamps can now be plated, in other words a specialist can now select a stamp and identify the actual printing plate and the position on a printing plate from which it came. This of course increases the demand for the stamps and has a natural affect on the price. Apart from the first and second issues of Holland, namely the 1852 to 1863 and 1864 issues, those issues of 1867 to 1871 are also extremely interesting with their numerous dies and perforations, and in fact it is extremely difficult to attempt to complete these issues unused, which of course has an affect on the price and subsequently is interesting from the investment point of view.

The next country that comes to my mind is Norway. The first stamp of Norway issued in 1855 which was a 4 skilling value and imperforate, would have been selling for around £4 ten years ago in used condition and now similar stamps are worth £45. The Norway No. 1 as it is called has great interest from a collector's and specialist's point of view. It is rather like the 1d Black of Great Britain in so much that it is a stamp which is attractive to specialists, and has proved fairly simple to plate, but unlike the 1d Black there are only four plates from which it was printed. This reconstruction of the plates is rewarding to the collector and gives him the thrill of searching among stamps to complete his plates.

The Oscar I stamp of 1866 and the two issues of Lions of 1863 and 1867 are particularly sought after and will always prove a good investment. The 3 skilling value of both issues is the most popular and the most sought after. Even the later issues up to 1875 are interesting and much sought after from the collector's point of view which in its turn must have an affect on the investing side.

From Norway we now turn to France, which is an extremely interesting country philatelically speaking and in some ways comparable to Great Britain. There is a great scope and variety in French stamps and they are generally available throughout the world. In attempting to form a collection or portfolio of French stamps one must be prepared to pay high prices. They are very beautiful stamps and have always been popular, and amongst the stamps of France are many great rarities. Naturally the first issue of this country is in the forefront when it comes to investing, but there is also a demand for the Bordeaux issues of 1870, which is so called because the stamps were issued in Bordeaux during the Franco-Prussian war and are associated with the siege of Paris.

The market is very strong in the 'classic' stamps of Germany. These stamps are collected all over the world, as are the other countries I have mentioned, because one has only to realise that in the USA, Australia and other parts of the world emigrants from these countries have now settled, thereby spreading the demand of what was once their home country. But to return to Germany, the stamps have been very well studied and there is a mass of literature available to help the beginner, and naturally when there is a strong specialist demand,there is a strong investment market. The most interesting and valuable stamps of Germany are amongst the German States, which issued their own stamps prior to 1872. Amongst these, the stamps of Bremen are far more difficult to collect used, as opposed to unused; the first three stamps of Brunswick are a great rarity unused, and the stamps of Hanover are far scarcer in mint or unused condition, than used. Lubeck is another country like Bremen where used copies of some stamps are almost impossible to find. Prussian stamps are generally more popular used, although scarcer in mint condition, but of all the German States a collection of unused stamps of Wurtemburg is probably the most difficult to form.

Amongst the individual stamps which quickly come to my mind when considering rarity value and consequently investment, I would mention Bavaria 1849 1 kreuzer black and the 1 kreuzer grey-black, Brunswick the 1852 1 silbergrossen rose, the 2 silbergrossen blue and the 3 silbergrossen vermilion, Hanover the 1851 groschen black on grey-blue in unused condition, Saxony the 1850 3 pfennige which has always been a popular stamp with wealthy collectors, the 1851 2 and 3 neugroschen and of course the rare error of colour of the same date which is the ½ neugroschen on pale blue, the colour of the 2 neugroschen.

Another country which comes to mind is Belgium which is probably the most underrated country in Europe at the moment, philatelically speaking of course. The first issues, already mentioned, of 1849 depicting Leopold I, known as the Epaulettes, are very attractive and highly specilized. Actually these are even less available than the first issues of Holland, but the prices of the Belgium stamps are on the same level as those of Holland owing to the demand. Anyone thinking of including these stamps in a collection or portfolio should try to find stamps with the portrait clear of the postmark, as this makes all the difference when assessing the value, as all too frequently fine stamps are marred by the obliterations. The unused stamps of this issue are rare, particularly with the original gum. The next two issues of Leopold I are less scarce than the first, but they are very interesting because of the many different cancellations, including those in red, blue and green.

In contrast to Belgium, the prices of Swiss stamps have gone so high that they are beyond many people's capacity, but have always been and still are very strong from the investment point of view, especially those of the cantonal administrations.

Turning from Europe to other parts of the world, the stamps of China have had a great upsurge of interest, demand and of course value since a rapproachment with the West, and the early dragon issues of this country are proving very fine from the investment point of view, particularly those with the wide setting.

From China we turn to Japan where the demand has always been extremely strong and the early issues are very fascinating and ideal from the specialist point of view. The stamps of this country have been amply covered by new handbooks.

The stamps of the United States have always been, and will always be in great demand, and good from the investment point of view. However moving south, the stamps of South America did fall out of popularity a few years back, but now it appears that they are coming back fast, so they should prove a good field for investment. In South America the most popular countries are Brazil, Chile and moving slightly north, Mexico.

Investment in Commonwealth Stamps

by John Farthing, Investment Director, Stanley Gibbons Limited

There are a number of factors to be considered when thinking of stamps as an investment. All affect the stamps of the Commonwealth.

Investment values in stamps are supported by the collector's market. Therefore a strong local demand for the stamps of a country is perhaps one of the most important factors to be taken into account. Countries in which two major areas take an interest have the advantage of this two-pronged demand for their stamps. Small countries enable the investor to secure a number of stamps forming a large proportion of the classic issues. The stamps of some countries may look undervalued at a particular time or some types of stamps may provide similar investment possibilities. Countries which are philatelically dead, i.e. they no longer issue stamps, are examples of one important aspect of stamp investment; supply cannot increase, but demand can and does.

A would-be investor may have an interest in one country or another. He may be historically minded or he may find plating, that is building up a complete original sheet out of stamps printed from the different positions on the plate interesting. In the Commonwealth there are so many possibilities and some difficulties that an investor needs the help of a reputable dealer.

Collecting stamps of the British Commonwealth has always been an attractive proposition particularly as so many collectors, especially in the UK are quite naturally biased towards the stamps of the former Empire. Moreover, the exquisite engraving of the earlier issues, their colours and the romance attached to so many have fascinated collectors and investors alike.

The stamps of the Australian states interest both collectors in the UK and those in Australia partly because some of them were locally produced from the start while others were printed in the UK and partly because of the increasing interest in things Australian on the part of Australians.

Again there is the strong continuing demand for Canadian stamps. Similarly both Rhodesians and South Africans are buying Rhodesian stamps.

Among the stamps of the Commonwealth there are examples of the other important factors in investment. People both in the United Kingdom and Europe take an interest in the stamps of islands like Cyprus, Malta and Gibraltar. There are a number of small countries such as Bermuda, the Falkland Islands and Mauritius of which the stamps are of great interest. In 1974 India and Malaya looked undervalued philatelically. The British North American Provinces, British Columbia and Vancouver Island, New Brunswick, Newfoundland, Nova Scotia and Prince Edward Island to name but a few no longer issue stamps. The 1d Black, the 2d Blue and the 1d Red are examples of stamps that can be plated and the stamps used during the Boer War and the envelopes to which they were affixed trace the history of that war. They show the areas from which the troops came to fight in the Boer War and the transports used. They also show how first the Boers invaded the British colonies of the Cape and Natal. They show, too, how the war against the British was conducted and trace the various seiges of Ladysmith, Mafeking and Fort Tuli. Envelopes from British soldiers held prisoner of war emphasised the success of the Boers during this period. But then envelopes and post marks show how it was the turn of the Boers to become prisoners of war as Lord Roberts and his great army began to move forward. They also show how the Boer prisoners were sent to the outposts of the then Empire as for example, Ceylon, India and St Helena. Then post-cards show President Kruger's retreat to Portugese East Africa.

There are, of course, an almost infinite number of examples of history shown in stamps. In the same way the development of countries like Rhodesia is revealed in the stamps and the postmarks on them.

But there are difficulties arising from the complexity of some Commonwealth stamps which emphasise the need for the advice of a reputable dealer.

The first stamps of New South Wales called Sydney Views for example were engraved in Sydney and could be described as somewhat primitive. These stamps however, are generally of more interest to specialist collectors owing to the complexity of the different printings, of the re-touching of the plates and of the different types of paper. Similarly, Victorian stamps which are probably the most complicated issues of all Australian States are not of so much interest to philatelists generally and possibly therefore, to investors. The stamps were lithographed by different printers and were printed in various conditions of the dies and even the same printing would have different lithographed stones and transfers. In the later issues there are no less than five very similar yet different watermarks consisting of a 'V' above a crown. There is, moreover a distinction between the two important series of Rhodesian stamps, the Double Heads and the Admirals. The latter form a rather complicated issue and although by 1974 prices were developing, the stamps could be more likely to remain the special concern of collectors than the attractive and simpler Double Heads, yet the Admirals could suit more modest pockets while the demand is growing and adequate supplies do not seem to be available in the market. In fact, although there is a great interest in all these stamps, it may be that investors should not concern themselves with them without consulting a reputable stamp dealer.

Investors will however principally consider the trend in prices. In general, demand for most British Commonwealth stamps from Queen Victoria to George VI has become increasingly strong. Stamps issued in the reigns of Queen Victoria and Edward VII increased by 25 per cent in twelve months before the issue of the Stanley Gibbons 1975 catalogue and those of George VIs reign by 20 per cent. These increases were larger in percentage terms than in the preceding twelve months. For investment there is therefore a very wide choice but the stamps selected are all important. Time and time again, superb quality has fetched well above the catalogue price. By the same token of course poor quality fetches only a fraction of catalogue value. This could also indicate the importance of advice from a reputable dealer specialising in classic stamps.

Precis of Relevant Information

1. Stanley Gibbons have always recommended "classics" (that is issues prior to 1900), and other material up to around 1930 which we consider to have good potential. The quality of the item plays an important part in our choice because it is only the best that commands a premium.

2. From our experience stamp investments are in the medium to long term category, say five to ten years, because initially our profit margin has to be absorbed. However in many cases our stamp portfolios rise immediately.

3. The only items we sell for investment are those that we feel we will untimately want to repurchase. Experience has show that by following our guidance stamp investors can make upwards of 12½% - 15% per annum.

4. We like our investors to take an interest in their stamps, and although this is by no means a prerequisite of our service we do pride ourselves on the high percentage of investors who turn into philatelists. Clients often win medals at exhibitions, thus adding to the value of the collection when sold. If you so wish we can offer advice on how your collection should be presented for an exhibition.

5. If you are not interested in philately, you keep the portfolio of stamps and we keep a photographic record so that if a collector wants an item you hold we contact you and if the price is tempting enough you sell. This happens quite often, frequently within a very short period.

6. Whilst the minimum investment is £500, it is possible to accept an initial lower figure as part of your investment plan.

7. If you and several friends want to invest a sum of money together, say £20,000, you can invest anything you like towards a grand total, subject to a minimum of £500 at a time.

8. We recommend that your stamps as an investment be kept in a safe at your home so that you

can browse through them and keep interested, or of course you can keep them at your bank. In cases where the investment exceeds £5,000 we are prepared for a small fee, which includes insurance, to store it for you in one of our vaults.

9. A portfolio contains a variety of selected specialized classic material such as single stamps, blocks, covers, proofs, and material of historic interest, or even a specialized collection. The number of items will of course vary according to your requirements.

10. You can sell all or part of your investment for cash whenever you wish. There is an international market for stamps in most countries of the world and London is recognised as the centre. Our object in selecting the finest material for you is that we hope to have the opportunity of repurchasing it at a later date.

BANKNOTES

PAPER MONEY – A NEW INVESTMENT?

Until the last few years notaphily was an obscure hobby with only a handful of dedicated collectors. Because interest in it is comparatively small, prices are still quite low. The old rule of thumb 'supply and demand' criteria comes into play. No matter how rare an item is, if the collector is even rarer the price is adversely affected. But with the hobby of collecting banknotes we find that while many of the notes are extremely rare, and the collectors are few, in comparison to stamp and coin collectors, it is a growing hobby.

The overall result is that the material is obtainable at low prices; even the semi-unique pieces usually being less than £1000, and that the investor is on to a very good bet indeed if the hobby matures. It is quite conceivable that collectors of paper money will double and treble in number within a matter of a few years. We are not now dealing with hundreds of thousands of existing collectors of, say, coins, but a few thousand. The popularity of the hobby is spreading — an ideal indication of this is the number of books and catalogues on the subject now being printed. It is a reasonable gamble that a few thousand more people will collect paper money during the next year or two. This means that more people will be after the rarities which only exist in very small quantities. The law of supply and demand will operate and prices will go up.

It has already been found that some notes thought to be common because a bunch of them turned up are in fact rare. What has happened is that the 'bunch' was absorbed at inexpensive prices and the dealers were then unable to replace them. Collectors, aware that no more were about, set the increase in value themselves when offering for sale their duplicates.

The investor has to decide for himself whether or not he thinks paper money is a sufficiently attractive hobby to entice more and more people to collect. Why, he might ask, did not people collect them before? The answer is that the majority of collector-minded people did not realise the potential. The pioneer collectors were in no hurry to publicise the hobby because if it caught on they would have to pay more for items they wanted to add to their collections. It was only really with the advent of a few books and catalogues mainly by George Sten and Albert Pick, that the hobby came into the limelight.

What then recommends pieces of old paper money to a collector? In the first place many of them are works of art in their own right. The finest engravers in the world were selected to design paper money for the simple reason that the issuers wanted it to be very difficult for anyone to forge them. Intricate designs executed by master-craftsmen were felt to be an assurance against forgery. The designs were made attractive because the issuers also had the problem of making people accept their notes instead of coins. Only in recent years has research started revealing some of the famous engravers responsible for what are in reality beautiful works of art.

Banknotes also have the advantage of being historically interesting. Early notes usually came into being because of emergencies: revolution, war, natural disaster. So one finds the notes signed by various great statesmen 'promising to pay'.

From the point of view of attracting new collectors paper money has as much, and often more, to commend itself as any other collecting hobby. Therefore it is an odds-on favourite to become a major hobby in future. Notaphily has already passed through the formative period when it spread from just a few hundred collectors to become an international hobby. Societies have been founded not just in the United States and Europe but in places like Columbia and Peru. A look at the membership lists of these societies shows how membership is growing rapidly.

Now let us take a look at a series of notes and see how an investor could expect to do well from them assuming that the hobby has a growth rate at least equal to other hobbies.

A good example is the series of notes issued during the Boer War, for here we have details of the exact amount of notes issued. Kruger issued notes from Pretoria dated May 28th, 1900. As Lord Roberts entered the town within a month of that issue it is fair to assume that the notes did not see a great deal of circulation. The most common of these issues is the £1 second type which one catalogue prices at as little as £2.50 in circulated condition and £15 in extremely fine condition. Yet only 11,000 of these notes were issued. If we now go to the scarcest note in the set, the £100 note, we will find that only 800 were issued and catalogues in 1972 were listing it at about £40 in circulated condition. Even if all 800 notes still exist it does not take much imagination to see how quickly they could all be absorbed in the collecting world.

The next issue of Kruger notes are even scarcer. These were issued at Pietersburg between February and April of 1901 when, once again, Kruger's forces were obliged to leave as British troops took over the territory. We find the £50 and £100 issues were limited to 150 each. Yet only a year or two ago these were being priced at around £200 in perfect condition. It is not inconceivable that 150 new collectors will come along in one year and absorb the lot!

The investor who likes his notes to have historical association will find the third and last issue of Kruger notes by far the most interesting. These are the notes known as the 'Te Velde' series. They were issued by the military 'in the field'. President Kruger had been ousted from all major towns and this last issue of notes was produced at Pilgrims Rest, a small mining town in the Eastern Transvaal. They were fairly crude because of the circumstances of their issue. They were printed on school exercise book paper, complete with lines and a small portable press was operated by the same men who in better times had minted Kruger's gold coinage. The most issued of any one note was 6,500 (The £1 dated May 1st 1902) but most issues were down to a few hundred of each. Even so they were being catalogued at under £100 each. Clearly there is a good investor's market in these notes. The same, however, can be said for a large number of different types of banknotes of the world.

There is a great deal of research to be done in the banknote-world. Even quite modern notes sometimes turn up that are uncatalogued and unknown. Such items give spice to the hobby, give the investor a chance to make a good discovery and make it the more attractive to collectors. It has been said by several professionals that while they can take hold of a piece of silver 2000 years old, date it, even tell one the engraver's name, etc a piece of paper money only a hundred years old can often confound the experts altogether!

Clearly the investor should learn something of the history of banknotes. There are many good books now on the market which serve as introductions to both collectors and investors. There are also a number of societies worth joining.Here one can meet collectors of varying interests and find out exactly what is popular and what is not.

The clever investor finds an area which is unpopular and buys up the material at inexpensive prices and waits for it to become popular. Then he is sitting on a gold-mine. Unfortunately it is not always the case that an unpopular area will become popular.

It is necessary to examine the reason for an area being unpopular. Sometimes it is found that banknotes of countries which do not use our language or alphabet are not popular simply because the average collector would prefer to go for something he can read or easily translate. Translating German, French, Spanish can be done comparatively easily with a good dictionary — but the moment the collector comes up against the Russian alphabet, or Arabic, he is faced with major problems.

Ironically, Chinese banknotes are among the most popular of all: but it must be remembered that many of them have the English language on them as well as Chinese characters and, perhaps above all, China has the romantic connection of being the first country to issue paper money, its first notes being attributed to 650 AD.

So in theory at least an investor can expect to make collections of Russian, Turkish etc., notes certainly less expensively than those of his own country or English speaking territories. While it is true that a Turk could say the same about English notes (and incidentally rare Turkish notes can fetch many hundreds of pounds in Turkey) statistically it becomes clear that far more collectors will be interested in English speaking territories than the banknotes of any other language.

If then, the investor can foresee a time when collectors will have no difficulty in understanding the banknotes issues of Russia and Turkey it is a reasonable supposition that they will become more popular among collectors.

We can see how this has already happened with China. Instead of an alphabet of twenty-six letters, China has something in excess of 40,000 characters. One could not imagine a more complicated language to deal with for a collector. Yet authors like George Sten and Brian Maltravers have successfully produced listings which will enable a collector to identify any Chinese banknote.

It is only a matter of time before Russian and Turkish notes are catalogued in the English language in such a way that a new collector can identify any note. Once this happens the value of the whole series will increase enormously.

Most collectors like to have reference works and catalogues so if a series of notes is not backed by such books it is not normally popular.

South American countries were in little demand a few years ago. There were no catalogues and the average collector had no clue to the rarity of the odd notes that turned up. The result was that very rare South American notes could often be bought for a few pounds whereas their counterparts in European countries were already fetching over a hundred pounds. Investors who moved into that area have already done well. At least seven books have gone onto the market within three years and a society was formed for collectors of these notes. To-day they are much more popular but it is worth noting that South American notes with certain exceptions are still comparatively inexpensive. There is probably a lot of room for the investor.

Sometimes even though there are catalogues and reference works notes do not appreciate in value to the extent that would interest an investor. It is important to study these notes and find out why. Two series of notes spring to mind. The Notgeld and inflation issues of Germany. Notgeld — emergency notes of the towns and cities of Germany during and following the 1914-18 war — were once very popular and German collectors would write to town halls to buy sets of notes as they came out. Special albums were produced. The result was that a town would find it could make quite an income from its fractional notes which, after all, only cost them the paper they were printed on. Some towns produced new sets, not because more notes were needed but to satisfy the collectors market. Other towns went to extremes and issued long sets illustrating the notes with fairy tales or the history of their town. With more than 100,000 such notes in existence the Reichsbank finally stepped in and prevented further issues by law. Even then a few cities managed to evade the legalities and produce 'specimens' and unissued notes. One or two towns ignored the law outright and continued until legal action was taken against them.

One must remember that as well as towns and cities, factories, shops and even police stations issued notes. The notes of 1914 were without question genuinely needed to offset the sudden shortage of small change due to hoarding. But by the end of the war there was not such a desperate need and before the issues ceased there was no need for them at all. Because a great many of these notes had been produced for collectors rather than for currency, the 'boom' collapsed and they fell in value. Only in the last few years has there been a resurgence of interest — allied to some excellent catalogues which are gradually setting out to catalogue the entire lot.

So an investor in the 1920s would have lost a lot of money in such a series — and quite a few did. It would be wrong to suppose that they are not worth bothering with. For one thing it is a series that young collectors can easily take to, where a lot of notes can be accumulated for little cost. Any collecting hobby can be likened to a pyramid financially. At the top thousands of pounds are paid for rarities but the top rests on an enormous base of collectors who perhaps cannot afford or don't wish to pay high prices and prefer more common notes. Take the base away and the top collapses.

There will always be an interest in Notgeld for the reason that the small income collector can enjoy himself studying them. It is also true that some Notgeld is rare and in demand. Notes of towns which changed hands during the war, towns which changed countries due to boundary alterations carry a premium. Some were issued for warships such as the *Hindenburg* (and these can fetch many pounds). The majority, however, are readily available for a few pence and while they are quite likely to go up in value they are not so likely to go up in the way that an investor would hope and would expect other series to do.

Two factors emerge which should instruct the investor. One, there were so many notes issued that collectors saw little hope of completion and two, they were not always issued for the genuine purpose of serving as currency.

Inflation notes of Germany can still be purchased in bundles at a few pence each. As with all types of notes one can always find rare and interesting ones. It would be wrong to suggest that all German inflation notes are common. The Billion denominations in particular fetch a lot of money and the 100 billionen has sold for several hundred pounds. But at the other end boxes full of million denominations are still around. In this case it was simply a case of too many notes being issued. When one considers that around ninety printing works were employed to print the paper money at the same time one can see how the nation was literally flooded with issues. The Reichsbank had been unable to cope with the demand for paper notes and had to get other printers to help. Again, towns and cities, unable to get supplies quickly enough, printed their own. Employees were given time off during the day to go and buy their shopping before prices increased again. Sometimes they were paid two and three times a day instead of weekly as a weeks pay would become valueless within days.

Other countries also suffered inflation and one sees enormous quantities of paper money for certain periods of time in Russia, China, Greece, Hungary etc. For the purpose of investment they cannot be such good bets as notes which are not available in quantity. Many collectors of course find them a very satisfying area of study and can build up large collections without ever paying more than about 25p a note.

There are other notes to be wary of. Normally one can say that any specimen note is a good investment. It is a good investment because a limited number were issued by the major security printers like De La Rue, Waterlows, Bradbury Wilkinson etc: usually about 600. But a number of 'specimen' notes have appeared on the market which are obtainable in much larger quantities. Czechoslovakian notes, many of them quite beautifully engraved and attractive to collectors, will be seen on the market perforated 'Specimen'. These are not true specimens at all but excess stocks of notes which the government finally put on the market for collectors cancelled by the perforation 'Specimen'.

Quite a number of East European countries seem to be affected. Notes of Bulgaria turn up in enormous quantities which suggest that obsolete issues were reprinted or printed in quantities quite unnecessary. This can happen also because of a sudden change of government as with Indonesia, where again certain issues were invalid overnight and available in large quantities.

On rare occasions a government may actually be party to producing notes for collectors. This is believed to have happened with the Che Guevara notes of Cuba. Being the only notes in the world actually signed with a nickname 'Che' and being issued by such a famous revolutionary the notes naturally attracted a lot of attention in the collecting world. Then Cuba began re leasing 'specimens' in large quantities. The position has arisen that the issued note is scarce and fetches several pounds while the 'specimens' are common.

As a general guide to investors on paper money the following criteria will be safe despite exceptions to it:

1 The item should have been produced for its original purpose ie if a banknote, for the purpose of circulating as currency, if a proof or specimen for the purpose of serving as examples to the authorities concerned with its issue like printers, the bank who ordered the issue and the Central Banks who need to know what issues have been made, etc. If the items have been produced for the collectors' market they should be treated as suspect.

2 If the items exist in large quantities like inflation notes they are clearly not going to appreciate in value to the same extent that are notes where only a few come onto the market.

3 The notes should have something to commend them to collectors. Either they should be attractive miniature works of art collectable for the vignettes on them, or they should be historically interesting. Perhaps they were signed by a famous person, issued for a siege or one of the earliest notes of that particular country. A note design of indifferent artistic merit on a note issued under normal conditions in a country requiring large quantities because of its big population is not likely to appeal as much as a beautiful or historically interesting note.

EARLY NOTES

A great many of the early issues of paper money contain hand-signed signatures. This means that as well as the historical reason for issue the notes have the added attraction of being signed by someone famous and a double-collectors interest in that autograph hunters are also interested.

With these early notes it is also possible to add to their value by researching them and unearthing data about their issue. For example the Khartoum notes issued by General Gordon include many containing his handwritten signature. An entry can be found in his journal stating: 'I offered in paying the three months *Backsheesh* to the troops, to give orders for bulk sums, £120, £130 but they refused to accept them, they want regular paper money, so I have issued £10,000 more in £50 notes. In this paper money I am personally responsible for the liquidation and anyone can bring action against me, in my individual capacity, to recover the money, while in the orders it might be a query whether they (the authorities in Cairo) might not decline to pay the orders. Paper cannot be bought at a discount, people have tried to buy it up, but have failed.'

It was thus possible to establish that only 200 £50 notes had been issued. Very few are known to exist and in 1974 one sold for about £1000.

A banknote does not necessarily have to be old to be valuable. There are many notes of the Second World War which command high prices because of their interest. Prisoner of War notes are particularly popular; concentration camps like Buchenwald and Theresienstadt have their own issues. Hundreds of different notes were produced in the Philippines by Guerilla forces. Perhaps the rarest of all the Second World War issues is the famous 2k of the German occupation of Ukraine. The rest of the set including the high denominations is quite inexpensive—a matter of a few pounds. But the 2k is worth well over

£1000. What happened was that the train carrying the consignment of the 2 denomination from Germany to the Ukraine was attacked by partisans, blown up and the notes scattered. German military retaliation was swift and thorough. In case the partisans had pockets full of the notes, the 2k was withdrawn before it had officially been put into circulation. The note consignment scattered by the railway lines was picked up note by note and burned. The area was then combed for partisans and anyone remotely suspect of being involved was executed. Only two of these notes have come to light though experts in German currency believe it possible for five to have survived. Such was the German thoroughness in accounting for the issue.

South American countries have particularly violent histories of war and revolution and much of this is traceable through their note issues. Here is a very good field for investment because only very recently have collectors become aware of the history behind the note. It was just not general knowledge among collectors for example that in the 19th Century Colombia suffered forty revolutions and ten civil wars culminating with the famous Thousand Day War. Many notes were issued by the various combatants. Some are obvious because of the war-like vignettes such as the improvised notes of the Liberals in the thousand day war which show a canon and a soldier with flag. The Liberals had become short of money and on the suggestion of Rafael Uribe Uribe, a general under Santos, issued notes to the troops.

There is still much research to be done into South American notes. In Peru Captain Guillermo Cervantes who commanded a battalion of Iquitos suddenly led a revolt against the government. It never stood much of a chance and in fact within four months government forces descended on the place in a well co-ordinated attack and ended the revolt. But Cervantes issued his own notes behind him.

Mexico is another territory which has left a maze of interesting banknotes from its civil war era. Among the paper issues are some bearing the name of General Francisco Villa — better known to schoolboys as the bandit chief Pancho Villa. The Mexicans called the notes *Las Sabanas de Villa* (Villa's sheets). The bandit chief Zapata in the southern and central states of Mexico was also financing his efforts with cardboard issues, but over-issue led to loss of confidence and Zapata then decided to issue notes headed *Banco Revolucionario de Guerrero*. The only thing wrong with these notes was that no such bank actually existed.

It would seem that when the American Revolution broke out many of the States still felt that a reconciliation with Britain was possible and desirable. For although they now considered themselves free agents and not obliged to take notice of British regulations for note issues a number of colonies, Pennsylvania, New Jersey, and Delaware referred to the reign of George III in the text of the notes and many of the new States retained the British coat of arms for sometime.

Maryland was first to issue a hard-line propaganda note against the British with its issue of July 26th, 1775. These notes depict George III trampling on the Magna Carta and setting fire to an American town. In Massachusetts Paul Revere engraved the motto 'Issued in Defence of American Liberty' and showed a Minute Man armed with a sword. At the same time the revolutionaries began switching from British monetary denominations to Spanish dollars — a practice already started before the revolution by Maryland.

The Continental Congress issued its own notes and the depreciation of these was such that the expression 'not worth a Continental' still lingers today.

These early American notes are probably one of the best investments today and many of them have been grossly undervalued by American collectors in the past. A very fine work exists on these issues entitled *The Early Paper Money of America* by Eric P. Newman

One of the most interesting series of early hand-signed notes of the world are those of the United States in the days when they were British colonies. The earliest known notes of America come from Massachusetts and were approved for issue on December

10th, 1690, which date appears on the notes. £7000 worth of these notes were issued in order to pay the military expenses for the war against Canada. The seal shows an Indian with the Latin inscription for 'Come over and Help us'. The British kept a tight rein on the issue of notes, and despite an urgent need for them, suppressed many issues.

Most of those that were authorised by the colonial power were issued to finance war. King George's war of 1741 to 1748, the French and Indian war 1754-63 and expeditions from New England against Louisburg. In the west the Indians aided by the French caused a lot of trouble and at various times Pennsylvania, New Jersey, Delaware, Maryland and Virginia found it necessary to issue paper bills to help finance military operations against them.

Virginia issued tobacco bills in 1713. The economy of the colony was based on tobacco and certificates were given to individuals who deposited their tobacco in the public tobacco warehouses. These tobacco certificates were readily negotiable and sufficed for the colonies' needs right up to 1755 when the colony finally issued normal paper money.

Some very interesting and famous people were concerned with the production of these early notes of America. Apart from such people as Benjamin Franklin and Paul Revere, there were well known silversmiths like Jeremiah Dummer, Nathaniel Hurd and John Coney engraving bills.

At this time notes were all hand-signed by famous people in order that the general public would accept them in lieu of coin. Colonial period notes are well worth close examination for any of the following signatures:
Signatories of the Declaration of Independence:

Abraham Clark
George Clymer
William Ellery
John Hart
Francis Hopkinson
Philip Livingston
John Morton
George Walton
James Wilson

Signatories of the Articles of Confederation:

Andrew Adams
William Ellery
Edward Langworthy
John Mathews
Daniel Roberdeau
Jonathan Baird Smith
Edward Telfair

Delegates to the Stamp Act Congress:

Joseph Borden
Metcalfe Bowler
Hendrik Fisher
Christopher Gadsden
Philip Livingston
Robert R. Livingston
Leonard Lispenard
Thomas Lynch
John Morton
John Rutledge

Signatories of the United States Constitution:

John Blair
David Brearley
William Few
Nicholas Gilman
William Jackson
Thomas Miffin
Charles Pinckney
Charles Cotesworth Pinckney
Edmund Randolph
John Rutledge
James Wilson

In practice most of the people who signed these early notes came from famous American families and have interesting stories behind them. There are notes, for example, signed by Lieutenant John Mease. He was the Lieutenant who with a small detail of men kept the camp fires burning brightly across the Delaware River while Washington's armies crossed over and came up behind the unsuspecting British forces to defeat them.

Forgeries of these early notes are often worth very much more than the genuine examples. The British set about forging notes with the idea of breaking the economy. In 1778 James Smither of Philadelphia was accused of counterfeiting Continental Currency for the British.

If The United States can claim the first authorised issue of paper money of North America, Canada can claim an early issue of 'paper' money as such. As early as 1685 Jacques de Meulles, Intendant of New France, found himself unable to pay his troops in coin. Paper was also short, so he used playing cards which were felt to be more durable in any case. The date and denomination were written on the back of the cards and they were hand-signed by the Governor and the Intendant and counter-signed by the Clerk of the Treasury as they were issued.

For small denominations cards were cut into halves and quarters while high denominations were issued as whole playing cards. These cards had to be redeemed within a year and the penalty for retention was death. It is not thought that any of these have survived. However, the economic situation did not improve and subsequent issues were made, later issues being on plain white cardboard. The Bank of Canada have some sixteen different types of card money of this period in their collection.

The battle of Quebec ended French sovereignty in Canada and the French Government then refused to honour their outstanding issues of card notes. Finally the British Government redeemed them at twenty-five per cent of face value.

INVESTING IN BRITISH BANKNOTES

The banknotes of Great Britain form a fascinating series and can be divided into several groups. The most notable of these is probably the Bank of England. Founded in 1694, the Bank of England is the pivot of British economy. It is the greatest banking institution ever created and today enjoys the trust and confidence that gave rise to the expression 'As safe as the Bank of England'.

When the Bank issued its first notes in 1694 they did not even have the status of legal tender. In its early history there were times when it had to suspend payment (notably the Napoleonic wars) and when its notes were actually discounted. But today every note ever issued by the Bank is redeemable — though not necessarily legal tender.

Lord Macaulay wrote of the Bank of England: 'It was.. not easy to guess that a Bill which purported only to impose a new duty on tonnage for the benefit of such persons as should advance money towards carrying on the war was really a Bill creating the greatest commercial institution that the world has ever seen.'

During the reign of William and Mary more money was needed to wage war with France. A Scotsman, William Paterson produced the idea which was drafted into a Bill 'for granting to Their Majesties several Rates and Duties upon Tonnages of Ships and vessels and upon Beer, Ale and other Liquors; for securing certain Recompenses and Advantages in the said Act mentioned to such persons as shall voluntarily Advance the sum of Fifteen Hundred Thousand Pounds towards carrying on the War against France.'

The promoters' 'recompenses and advantages' were that they could raise £1,200,000 and create a Corporation to be named 'The Governor and Company of the Bank of England'. The capital was to be lent to the Government at eight per cent interest.

The investor should not overlook the modern notes and particularly when keeping up to date with new issues will always have the satisfaction of knowing that they retain their face value all the time. Some modern notes are rare already, like the 1961 issue of O'Brien with the letter 'R' found in the white space above the lower 'Bank of England' on the reverse side of the note. All known notes have the prefix letters AOIN to AO6N. They identify the notes as having come from an experimental machine. It is estimated that only 5 million were printed which represents about 0.49 per cent of the 1,120 million new £1 notes issued in 1961. As collectors were not aware of this variety until after printing had ceased the 'R' condition notes are very rare, fetching as much as £60.

Serial prefix letters are important as in some cases there was a signature change half way through the serial letters, and some letters were used for 'replacement notes' (replacing damaged or error notes during printing).

A list of these serial prefixes is produced on pages 87 to 89 to show the differences and the investor might well consider that a complete collection would not be too difficult to form and would obviously be worth much more as a complete collection than would a comprehensive collection.

The next section of British notes would be the Treasury Notes. These came about through the hoarding of gold and silver in the Great War of 1914-18. Under the 1833 Act, Bank of England notes were legal tender only for amounts of over £5. The 1914 Currency and Bank Notes Act, passed on August 5th (the day after war was declared) allowed the Treasury to issue its own notes. The August Bank Holiday was extended for three clear days while the Treasury rushed through the printing. Paper was in short supply and the Treasury had to resort to stamp paper watermarked with the Royal Cypher (Simple) for the first issue. These were quickly nicknamed "Bradburys" after Sir John Bradbury, permanent secretary to the Treasury. Issued on August 14th, 1914 they were badly printed and were soon to be replaced with the August 7th issue.

A number of different issues were subsequently made including the famous Arabic overprint notes issued to British soldiers on the Dardanelles Campaign. The £1 is undoubtedly one of the best investment items in the Treasury series and will fetch over £200.

Scottish banknotes form an extensive series and for the investor a very good series. They are the most colourful and attractive of all the British notes and they range in denominations from £1 to £100. Many of the £1 notes of the early 1900s are large square notes which are always popular with collectors. Many different banks issued notes depicting a wide range of subjects. Although well collected it is thought by many notaphilists that once a definitive catalogue appears on the market listing the range of notes a great many more collectors will be created. This appears to be the effect of a first-time catalogue in any collecting field so from the investors' point of view Scottish notes are a very good field as it is almost certain that a comprehensive catalogue of Scotland will be published shortly.

Another series of British notes which is always safe for investment is the private and Joint Stock Banks. At one time more than 900 such banks were in operation issuing their own notes. Most of these banks fell by the wayside during economic upheavals. In 1825 the failure of Sir Peter Cole and Company led to sixty-three banks collapsing and it was not until the Bank Charter Act of 1844 introduced by Sir Robert Peel that private banks were effectively restricted in their note issues — the Act also gave a monopoly to the Bank of England for issuing notes within a radius of sixty-five miles of London. Private banks gradually decreased and in 1921 when Fox, Fowler and Co, of Wellington, Somerset, amalgamated with Lloyds Bank, the last English private banknotes came to an end. However, the Isle of Man continued issuing private notes up until 1961.

Only a handful of these private banks have left behind large numbers of their issues. Most of the banks are scarce and usually only half a dozen or so notes turn up every now and then of each bank and are quickly absorbed by the growing band of collectors.

No comprehensive list of these banks has ever been published before but Mr James Douglas, Scottish archivist has compiled the list on page 115 which is a major step towards a complete cataloguing of all private banks of England.

The investor will note that in many cases the authorised circulation of the banks was very small — by comparison to modern bank issues very tiny indeed. He has to decide how many of the authorised circulation are still available in order to find the better investments. Where a bank is known to have gone into bankruptcy it is a fair bet that a number of its notes were left unredeemed but where the bank merged with the major banks like Midlands, Lloyds, Barclays, National Westminster it means that the notes would still be redeemed today if presented to the banks. The likelihood of many surviving is remote as people did not keep such notes. A £1 note in the 1880s was a lot of money and a £5 note was in some cases a year's wages for a maid.

The better type of private note is already in high demand and the stories behind the individual banks are sometimes so fascinating that collectors are likely to increase considerably once information about these notes is made more widespread.

Long term investors may also consider the Irish notes to be a sound investment. At the moment, probably because of the political problems, Irish notes are not in great demand in Britain. In consequence they are inexpensive by comparison. The investor who is confident that all will be resolved well may consider that now is the time to get together an assortment of the bank note issues.

As in the stamp world where the classics of any country have always lived up to investors' expectations, so in the banknote world the classics have so far shown themselves to be gilt-edged. The goldsmith notes — which can be traced back to the reign of Elizabeth I fetch between £100 and £500 when they appear on the market. So do the Exchequer Bills which were the first form of Legal tender payment by bills made in England.

1928 to date

There are two ways to tackle the acquisition of a definitive English collection.

1. *Type Face Collecting.* This means acquiring one of every note which differs in size, colour, signature or denomination. This is best done by reference, in the first instance, to the "Stanley Gibbons' Catalogue".

Bank of England notes are identified by prefix, that is the combination of letters and numbers preceding the main serial number, e.g. LNoNo equals Letter Number Number, e.g. A01. The complete list of prefixes and varieties of the Bank of England series of one pound and ten shilling notes since 1928 you will find set out on these tables taken from the collection held by David Keable for collectors reference. You will notice that on the pounds table most main series start with "A" or "A" in combination.

On the ten shilling table notice that the main series of the Brittania notes start with "Z" save for the presentation inaugural issue A01 and where a change of cashier produces a linking prefix. The portrait series (1960) starts with A01 as the first prefix of issue.

2. *First and Last Collecting.* Here the collector will seek to acquire the first and the last prefix of issue of every signature change. Such a collection will, of course, include all the scarce linking notes.

These occur where the Chief Cashier retires and a new signatory appears, then scarce varieties show (these are called linking prefixes). See £1 H30 Mahon linking at around H33 to Catterns. You may assume that "H" Catterns was issued to H99, thus "H" Mahon is a scarce and desirable note, sharing only one third of the issue of 100 million.

Replacement Notes are high desirables to a first and last collector. These are the notes put in the batches by the Inspector when a faulty note is found. They are scarce and are all linking notes, see M01/18 O'Brien to M56/80 Fforde on the ten shilling table. For some of the earlier series the notes themselves in any prefix are so scarce that the replacement notes have yet to be identified positively. Such a one is ten shilling Peppiatt LNoNo, A01 - 99.

A First and Last Collector would wish to include every prefix of "G" note in his collection, see the Stanley Gibbons Catalogue in the first instance. Otherwise you will find all known "G" notes noted on the issue chart. These were printed on the experimental Goebbels machine and the letter "G" will be found inset on the reverse at the bottom over Bank of England.

The scarcest modern note of all is the well known "R" research note. This carries a small "R" on the reverse in the same position as the "G". It has been recorded only from A01N — A06N. Linking to it (see under Hollom) is the first "G" note A01/99N "G" Hollom.

The "G" series itself produced a very scarce variety. The replacement "G", see M01/28N "G" Hollom, linking to M29/34N "G"

Experienced Collectors of stamps and coins will know that scarce issues and varieties bought early are top investments. All English notes in high grade are scarce. No large stocks exist. The older issues of the Brittania type were withdrawn and burnt by the Bank of England ten years before banknote collecting started in Great Britain. The English series 1914 - to date will prove to be the scarcest collector series in the world.

Mahon (LNoNo)	Catterns (LNoNo)	Catterns (NoNoL)	Peppiatt (NoNoL)	Peppiatt (War)	Peppiatt (War)	Peppiatt (War)	Peppiatt (LNoNoL)	Peppiatt (LNoNoL)	Peppiatt (LNoNoL)	Beale (LNoNoL)	Beale (LNoNoL)	Beale (LNoNoL)	O'Brien (LNoNoL)
A01		08 --A 99		01 A--D	05 A--E	04 A--H	10 A--A		34 A--B		03 A--C	11 A--J	
16 A--		?--B	17 --B	B--D	B--E	B--H	B--A		B--B		B--C	B--J	
B--			--C	C--D	C--E	C--H	C--A		C--B		C--C	C--J	
C--			--D	D--D	D--E	D--H	D--A		D--B		D--C	D--J	
D--	33		--E	E--D	E--E	E--H	E--A		E--B		E--C	E--J	
E--	H--		--H	H--D	H--E	H--H	H--A		H--B 36 ---	38 H--B	H--C	H--J	
F--	J--		--J	J--D	J--E	J--H	J--A			J--B	J--C	J--J	
G--	K--		--K	K--D	K--E	K--H	K--A			K--B	K--C	K--J	
	L--		--L	L--D	L--E	L--H	L--A 35			L--B	L--C	L--J 63	65 L--J
H-- 30	M--		--M	M--D	M--E	M--H	M-A N-A O-A?		Replacement Notes	M--B	M--C		M--J
	N--		--N	N--D	N--E	N--H	1948 printing			N--B	N--C		N--J
	O--		--O	O--D	O--E	O--H	14-15cm block		02 S--S 09	O--B	O--C	Replacement Notes	O--J
	R--		--R	R--D	R--E	R--H	01 R--A		(To Beale)	R--B	R--C	10 S--S 64	R--J
	S--		--S	S--D	S--E	S--H	01 S--A 35 ----------			S--B	S--C	(To O'Brien)	S--J
	T--		--T	T--D	T--E	T--H		41 S--A		T--B	T--C		T--J
	U--		--U	U--D	U--E	U--H		T--A		U--B	U--C		U--J
	W--		--W	W--D	W--E	W--H		U--A		W--B	W--C		W--J
	X--		--X	X--D	X--E?	X--H 93		W--A		X--B	X--C		X--J
	Y--		--Y	Y--D	Y--E?	Y--H?		X--A		Y--B	Y--C		Y--J
	Z-- 97		--Z 97	Z--D 81	Z--E?	Z--H?		Y--A		Z--B 64	Z--C 80		Z--J 98
								Z--A 99					

First Series

O'Brien (LNoNoL)	O'Brien (LNoNoL)	O'Brien (LNoNo)	O'Brien (NoNoL)	O'Brien (LNoNoL)	Hollom (LNoNoL)	Hollom (LNoNoL)	Hollom (LNoNoL)	Hollom (LNoNoL)	Hollom (LNoNoL)	Hollom (LNoNoL)	Hollom (LNoNoL)	Hollom (LNoNoL)	Fforde (LNoNoL)
22 A--K	14 A--L	01 A--	03 --A	01 A--N B 06	09 A--N G 99	07 A--R	A--S	A--T	A--U	A--W	A--X	01 A--Y 92	
B--K	B--L	B--	--B	01 B--N 76	77 B--N 99	B--R	B--S	B--T	B--U	B--W	B--X	01 B--Y 10	11 B--Y
C--K	C--L	C--	--C		C--N	C--R	C--S	C--T	C--U	C--W G	C--X		C--Y
D--K	D--L	D--	--D		D--N	D--R	D--S	D--T G	D--U	D--W	D--X		D--Y
E--K	E--L	E--	--E		E--N	E--R	E--S	E--T	E--U	E--W	E--X		E--Y
H--K	H--L	H--	--H	Hollom (LNoNo)	H--N	H--R	H--S	H--T	H--U	H--W	H--X		H--Y
J--IK	J--L 87	J--	--J		J--N	J--R	J--S	J--T	J--U	J--W	J--X		J--Y
K--K	08 K--L	K--	--K	Replacements	K--N	K--R	K--S	K--T	K--U	K--W	K--X		K--Y
L--K		L--	--L		L--N	L--R	L--S	L--T	L--U	L--W	L--X G		L--Y
M--K	Replacement	01 M--- 66 -------	--N	---- 69 M 99	01 M--N G 28	01 M--R 08	Replacement Notes					Fforde (LNoNoL)	
N--K	Notes	N--	--R	Hollom (NoNoL)		Links to M--N G Fforde						Replacements	
O--K	73 S--S 99	R--	--S	Replacements								29	
R--K	01 S--T 21	S--	--T	01 --M 99								M--G	
S--K		T--	--U									34	
T--K		U--	--W									09	
U--K		W--	--X									M--R	
W--K		X--	--Y									47	
X--K		Y--	96 Z										
Y--K		X 81											
Z--K 76													

ONE POUND
(Contd.)

Second Series

Fforde (LNoNoL)	Fforde (LNoNoL)	Fforde (LNoNoL)	Fforde (LNoNoL)	Fforde (LNoNoL)	Fforde (LNoNoL)	Fforde (LNoNoL)	Fforde (LNoNoL)	Fforde (LNoNoL)	Fforde (LNoNoL)	Replacements
A -- Z	N -- A	R -- A	S -- A	T -- A	U -- A	W -- A				
B -- Z	N -- B	R -- B G	S -- B	T -- B	U -- B	W -- B	X -- B			
C -- Z	N -- C	R -- C	S -- C	T -- C	U -- C	W -- C	X -- C			
D -- Z	N -- D	R -- D	S -- D	T -- D	U -- D					
E -- Z	N -- E	R -- E	S -- E	T -- E	U -- E G					
H -- Z	N -- H	R -- H	S -- H	T -- H						
J -- Z	N -- J	R -- J	S -- J	T -- J						
K -- Z	N -- K	R -- K	S -- K	T -- K						
L -- Z	N -- L	R -- L G	S -- L	T -- L						
				T -- M --- U -- M -- Replacements						
Replacements	N $\underset{14}{--}$ M G	R -- M	S -- M	T -- M G						

Page (LNoNoL)	Page (LNoNoL)	Page (LNoNoL)	Page (LNoNoL)	Page (LNoNoL)	Page (LNoNoL)	Page (LNoNoL)	Page (LLNoNo)
S $\overset{87}{--}$ L		U -- A	W -- A	X -- A	Y -- A	Z -- A	AN --
	T -- B	U -- B	W -- B	X -- B	Y -- B	Z -- B	BN --
	-- ?	U -- C	W -- C	X -- C	Y -- C	Z -- C	
R $\overset{47}{--}$ M	T -- D	U -- D	W -- D	X -- D	Y -- D		
S -- M	T -- E		W -- E	X -- E	Y -- E	Z -- H	
	T -- H	U -- H	W -- H	X -- H	Y -- H		
	-- ?	Replacements		X -- K	Y -- K		
	T -- K			X -- L	Y -- L		
	T -- L						

TEN SHILLINGS

Mahon (LNoNo) — *Unthreaded*
- A 01
- Z (01)
- Y - -
- X - -
- W - -
- V - - (to 11)

Catterns (LNoNo)
- V - - (14)
- U - -
- T - -
- S - -
- R - -
- O - -
- N - -
- M - -
- L - -
- K - - (to 97)

Peppiatt (LNoNo)
- J - - (01)
- H - -
- E - -
- D - -
- C - -
- B - -
- A - - (to 99)

Peppiatt (War) — *Threaded*
- Z (02) - - D/E - - (04)
- Y - - D/E - - (to 92)
- X - - D
- W - - D
- U - - D
- T - - D
- S - - D
- R - - D
- O - - D
- N - - D
- M - - D
- L - - D
- K - - D
- J - - D
- H - - D
- E - - D
- D - - D
- C - - D
- B - - D
- A - - D (to 78)

Peppiatt (NoNoL) — *Unthreaded*
- (01) - - Z
- - - Y
- - - X
- - - W
- - - U
- - - T
- - - S
- - - R
- - - O
- ? - - N
- ? - - M
- - - L (to 70)

Peppiatt (NoNoL) — *Threaded*
- (88) - - L
- - - K
- - - J
- - - H
- - - E (to 90)

Beale (NoNoL)
- (04) - - D
- - - C
- - - B
- (06) - - A (to 34)

Beale (LNoNoL)
- Z (01) - - Z
- Y - - Z
- X - - Z
- W - - Z
- U - - Z
- T - - Z
- S - - Z
- R - - Z
- O - - Z
- N - - Z
- M - - Z
- L - - Z
- K - - Z
- J - - Z
- H - - Z
- E - - Z
- D - - Z (to 85)

O'Brien (NoNoL)
- (36) - - A (to 67)

O'Brien (LNoNoL)
- D (86) - - Z
- C - - Z
- B - - Z
- A - - Z (to 93)

O'Brien (LNoNoL)
- Z (03) - - Y/X - - (04)
- Y - - Y/X - - (to 15)
- X - - Y
- W - - Y
- U - - Y
- T - - Y
- S - - Y
- R - - Y
- O - - Y
- N - - Y
- M - - Y
- L - - Y
- K - - Y
- J - - Y
- H - - Y
- E - - Y
- D - - Y
- C - - Y
- B - - Y
- A - - Y (to 97)

O'Brien (LNoNo) — *Portrait*
- A (01) - -
- B - -
- C - -
- D - -
- E - -
- H - -
- J - -
- K - - (to 62)
- M (01) - - (to 18)

Hollom (LNoNo)
- K (65) - -
- L - -
- M (19) - - (to 52)
- N - -
- R - -
- S - -
- T - -
- U - -
- W - -
- X - -
- Y - -
- Z - - (to 79)

Hollom (NoNoL)
- (01) - - A
- - - B
- - - C
- - - D
- - - E
- - - H
- - - J
- - - K
- - - L
- - - N
- - - R (to 23)

- Replacement Notes - M (56 to 80)

Fforde (NoNoL)
- (26) - - R
- - - S
- - - T
- - - U
- - - W
- - - X
- - - Y
- - - Z (to 94)

Fforde (LNoNoL)
- A (01) - - N
- B - - N
- C - - N
- D - - N (to 38)

PORTRAIT £5

Hollom (LNoNo)
- A (01) - -
- B - -
- C - -
- D - -
- E - -
- H - -
- J - -
- K - -
- L - -
- M (01?) - - Replacement
- N - -
- R - -

Fforde (LNoNo)
- M (18) - - Replacement
- R (20) - -
- S - -
- T - -
- U - -
- W - -
- X - -
- Y - -
- Z - - (to 97)

Fforde (NoNoL)
- (01) - - A?
- - - B
- - - C
- - - D
- - - E
- - - H?
- - - J?
- - - K?
- - - L (to 02)
- (01 to 10) M Replacement

Page (NoNoL)
- (26) - - C
- - - D
- - - E
- - - H
- - - J?
- - - K?
- - - L?
- (04 to 10) M Replacement

SOUTH AFRICAN BANKNOTES

by David Paterson

As the South African highveld has produced a Reef of Gold, influencing the world economy, so has the every-day business life of the country brought forth a golden opportunity for collectors and investors in the varied, interesting and historical banknote issues of the past and present. Although a comparatively young country, South Africa has always aroused a great deal of interest in other countries, and this has become particularly noticeable in the banknote collecting field. Even though the country became a republic outside the Commonwealth in 1961, many Commonwealth collectors continue to include the South African banknote issues in their collections.

The first banknotes, issued by the Dutch government, had to be hand-written as there was no printing press available. These were issued in Rix-Dollars, but it was found that they were easy to forge, so the printings were changed regularly. This paper money was introduced owing to a shortage of coin, only about £500 worth of metal money being available in the Cape at this time (1790). After the first British occupation, the Rix-Dollar paper money had depreciated by a quarter, and in 1804 all existing money was called in for replacement by the Batavian Government. Following the second British occupation of the Cape, some two million dollars in Rix-Dollars were in circulation, and in 1810 the notes were radically changed by having a new stamp impression of Britannia added. Although there was such a large amount of this paper money available at this time, not a great deal has survived to the present day, and these issues are scarce, as are all banknotes issued in Southern Africa during the first half of the 19th Century.

The currency of Great Britain replaced Cape money in 1831, all Rix-Dollars were called in, and these were replaced by promissory notes for £1, £5, £10, £50 and £100. The first bank set up in the Cape was a State bank, the Lombard Bank, established in 1793, and lasted until 1843. The first private bank was opened by Mr J B Ebden in 1837 after a false start in 1826, and was known as the Cape of Good Hope Bank. There were altogether some forty well established private banks in existence in South Africa before 1863, but most of these closed during the latter half of the 19th Century, and by 1893 only four were still operating.

Some of the notes from these early private banks have appeared on the market recently, for example the Bank of South Africa two Rix-Dollars note in proof form, which fetched more than £300. Another typical and interesting example is the £5 Montague Bank note of the Cape of Good Hope. This shows a vignette of John Montague, who was present at the Battle of Waterloo. A further well designed note is the Barry & Newphews £5 Swellendam type, showing an ox-wagon team, the traditional method of transport in those times.

Even the later banknotes of the latter 19th Century period are not often obtainable, but do become available from time to time. The old Transvaal Republican issues of 1868 are good examples, a banknote of this period recently realised about £300. The 1862 Colonial Bank of Natal issues have also been sold recently, at prices varying between £150 to £250.

The greatest field of interest, however, appears to be the Military and Emergency notes issued during the South African War period, between 1899 and 1902. These notes not only appeal to all South African collectors, but also to the steadily increasing numbers of those interested in Military History. A great deal of research has been conducted in the issues of this period, and our knowledge is growing. Among the well-known battles and sieges of the war, undoubtedly the most famous was the Siege of Mafeking, the defence of which town was conducted by the ledgendary Colonel R Baden-Powell. The siege began in October 1899, and lasted for 217 days, costing the British garrison 273 casualties in dead and wounded. The town was eventually relieved by a column led by Colonel Plumer. During the siege, every attempt was made to carry on as best as possible. Food rationing was introduced, a postal service organised, and when a shortage of coins arose, due to hoarding, Baden-Powell arranged with Mr R Urry (the Manager of the Standard Bank) for an issue of low denomination notes. These were first circulated during January 1900, for 1/—, 2/— and 3/— values, and bore the signature of Captain H Greener, Chief Paymaster to the garrison. A number of varieties exist on all these issues, which are of great interest to collectors.

It was found necessary to issue a 10/— and £1 note, and these appeared in March 1900. The 10/— note was printed from a woodcut, using a croquet mallet cut in half for the block, and is found in two types — with correct spelling and with the word 'commanding' spelled as 'commaning'. The error type is much sought after, and is priced at £10 more than the current note The £1 note was printed photographically by the ferro-prussiate process by Mr E C Ross, who managed to produce about twenty notes a day. The colour of these is found to vary between a very deep Prussian blue to a pale sky blue.

The rarities of these issues are the £1 and 3/— notes, and the value of these has shown a steady increase over the past couple of years. The approximate issue figures of all used types is as follows, with prices shown in VF+ condition. EF condition is scarcer, and is worth considerably more.

1 shilling	*6,950*	*£30-£50*
3 shillings	*850*	*£55-£75*
£1 blue, scarce	*683*	*£200-£275*
2 shillings	*5,700*	*£35-£55*
£10/- normal (and error)	*7,000*	*£35-£50*

Another interesting British issue to come from the war is the Upington Border Scouts issue. These notes were printed on cloth, with the name of the unit, due to a shortage of paper. The amounts were handwritten and handsigned by Major Birbeck. The denominations were shown in 2/—, 5/—, 10/—, and £1 and £2 amounts. A rare £5 issue has also come on to the market quite recently. These notes have also shown a steady increase in value, and now realise between £175 and £250 each.

Turning to the Boer side of the conflict, we find many interesting emergency issues. By 1900, due to the shortage of money, paper money was being printed in Pretoria by the Kruger Government. On May 28th of this year, the following denominations were issued: £1, £5, £10, £20, £50 and £100, all showing Pretoria as the place of issue. After the British occupied the town, the Transvaal government retreated to Pietersburg, where a new issue was made in identical denominations, dated 1st March, 1st April and 1st May 1902, with the name 'Pietersburg' printed in place of 'Pretoria'. These notes were not as well printed as the first series, being printed on stationery paper.

After the British forces overran the Pietersburg area, the Boers fled, taking the printing press with them. President Kruger travelled with this party, and later crossed the border into Portuguese East Africa, from where he sailed to exile in Europe. The last series of these notes were printed at a small Eastern Transvaal mining town, Pilgrim's Rest, and are known as the "Te Velde" issues, as they were printed in the field under military administration. They were printed on white ruled paper of the school-book type, and the original ruled lines are always seen on this type. Only three denominations were issued, £1, £5 and £10, and show three dates, 1st March, 1st April and 1st May 1902. The Peace Treaty was signed at Vereeniging on 31st May 1902.

There are a number of varieties seen on the ZAR notes, especially on the first (Pretoria) series. These can be identified by differences in the ornamental borders, (first and second types), and by the prefix 'No' missing (third type). These are known to be issued as follows (prices shown for VF+ condition).

£1	*type*	*1,*	*5,000*	*issued,*	*£10-£25*
£1	*"*	*2,*	*11,000*	*"*	*£7-£15*
£1	*"*	*3,*	*5,000*	*"*	*£12-£30*
£5	*"*	*1,*	*1,500*	*"*	*£35-£55*
£5	*"*	*2,*	*4,500*	*"*	*£10-£25*
£5	*"*	*3,*	*8,000*	*"*	*£15-£35*
£10	*"*	*3,*	*7,000*	*"*	*£9-£20*
£20	*"*	*1,*	*2,100*	*"*	*£15-£25*
£50	*"*	*1,*	*1,500*	*"*	*£19-£40*
£100	*"*	*1,*	*800*	*"*	*£60-£120*

£1	1.2.	1901	6,500	issued	£8-£20
£1	1.3.	1901	2,500	"	£10-£30
£1	1.4.	1901	49,500	"	£3-£7
£5	1.2.	1901	1,500	"	£20-£45
£5	1.4.	1901	4,500	"	£8-£25
£10	1.4.	1901	1,700	"	£14-£30
£20	1.4.	1901	800	"	£55-£150
£50	1.4.	1901	150	"	£150-£200
£100	1.4.	1901	150	"	£135-£200

£1	1.5.	1902	6,500	issued	£7-£25
£5	1.3.	1902	1,100	"	£25-£55
£55	1.4.	1902	400	"	£55-£110
£5	1.5.	1902	1,000	"	£12-£30
£10	1.3.	1902	500	"	£60-£130
£10	1.4.	1902	800	"	£30-£65
£10	1.5.	1902	800	"	£25-£55

There are a few notes known that have no signature or date. These are usually priced about £60 over the value of the signed issues. Some of the early issues can be found with the British 'Captured and Cancelled' overprint.

Following the war, various private banks in the four Provinces continued to issue local notes, but by 1920, following various take-overs, their numbers had dropped to four. The South African Reserve Bank was given the right to issue all bank notes in this year, by virtue of the Currency and Banking Act. All private notes prior to 1920 are therefore much sought after by collectors, and realise high prices.

The first South African Reserve Bank notes were issued in sterling, and were on a par with the British pound, until the country changed to the decimal system in 1961. The new issue in this year was based on a ten shilling unit, known as the rand. The colour of the new 1 Rand note remained the same as the old 10/— note, to assist the change-over. Likewise the old £1 note became the 2 Rand note, merely having the '1' denomination changed to '2', and the £5 to R 10.

Returning to the 1920-21 issues, these appeared in two languages, English and Dutch, which was changed to English and Afrikaans in 1928. All notes were dated until 1961, and all Reserve Bank notes bear the signature of the Governor at the time of issue. Thus there are many date and signature types for study, likewise the various colour changes and watermarks introduced over the years. This means additional interest for the specialist collector, and stimulates a healthy market.

COMMONWEALTH BANKNOTES

by Brian Kemp

With the Banknote collecting hobby in full sway the investor may well ask 'which countries are the best bet for me?' The British Commonwealth is in my opinion a series worth contemplating. There are some seventy territories involved. To collect this series is to unfold the stirring story of the growth of the British Empire which was, at its zenith, the greatest empire the world has ever seen. The specialist and the investor will have a wide and interesting field to cover and the knowledge gained will be of everlasting value.

Notes of Cyprus are very popular because few issues were needed for the small population, and today they are very hard to obtain. The George V series of notes from 1914 are very rare and when they do come on the market are immediately snapped up. The George V1 and more recent stirling issues of Queen Elizabeth II are now in great demand. These issues are becoming harder to find.

Issues of the West Indies can be a lifetime's study and new finds are turning up all the time. A note which came on the market recently, 'The Colonial Bank' $5 1882 issued for the Island of St Vincent is worth more than a thousand times its face value now because the note issue in those days was very limited and the population it served was mainly the rich middle class. The poor caribs were served by a very mixed coinage indeed.

The Colonial Bank was later taken over by Barclays Bank and this bank issued notes for the Islands, Dominica, Grenada, St Vincent, St Lucia and St Kitts. All these island issues are very hard to obtain and are worth investing in. A friend of mine recently picked up one of these notes from a dealer's cheap album for £2, which goes to show that with a little hunting good profits can be made.

Canada is also a very interesting area in which to specialise, although a warning must be given here for the novice and small investor whose pocket is limited. Some of these notes can cost a thousand pounds each.

Australia is another area with notes that provide a glimpse into her early history. The acute shortage of coins made traders and merchants issue their own private notes. Many of the small size notes were nicknamed 'Shinplasters', due to habit of the populace putting them in their boots to hide them. The traders soon got wise to this and had the notes printed on paper designed to disintegrate after a time. Hence when the poor owner came to demand cash, his note was eroded and no-one would honour it. This practice could not, of course, continue and the Bank of New South Wales opened her doors in 1817. This great Bank continues to do business and is an integral part of Australian society.

The early notes of the bank are very rare and when they do appear command a very high price. The Pacific Islands are another area rich in the early history of the British Empire. Fiji issued notes in the 1870s. The first notes recorded are the notes prepared but not issued by Brewer and Foske, a private firm. One of these notes turned up recently in some personal belongings of Sir John Gorrie who travelled throughout the Empire and was associated with many banks. A book could be written on this very interesting gentleman. Cannibals still roamed these Islands in the 1870s and the Paper Money issues are an interesting story of the transition from outright savagery to a civilized community.

New Zealand notes were also very scarce in the 19th Century. The early 20th Century issues are hard to obtain as well. Notes worth looking for in the modern series are the Replacement issues. These are notes which are used to replace any damaged or faulty notes and the replacement is immediately recognised by an asterisk before the serial number. The British Solomon Islands notes appear from time to time. If any come the investor's way, and the price is reasonable, take them. They are 'blue chip' and will be very expensive in the future.

The note issues of South Africa reflect the history of this rich and colourful country. They begin with the Rix Dollar notes of the Cape of Good Hope in the early years of the 19th Century and pass through the transitional period of a young pioneer country with such notes as the Bank of Natal, The Durban Bank, and the National Bank. There is one fairly common issue of this period, the Montague Bank, featuring the founder of the Bank who fought at the Battle of Waterloo as a young lad of seventeen.

India is a country that has been left out in the cold by banknote collectors in the past, but is now becoming popular. The word is out of notes being issued during the Indian mutiny, I have yet to see these notes. The Bank of Bengal and the other presidential bank, The Bank of Bombay issued notes during this period. The Government notes of India with the portrait of Queen Victoria on them are very rare indeed now. Five years ago one could purchase them for a few pounds.

The George V issues make interesting study. There are many signatures and colour varieties to be found. The investor can also find interesting signature varieties in the later modern issues of India. The many small islands scattered throughout the former Empire are rich hunting grounds for the shrewd investor.

Cocos and Keeling Islands with their small population of less than a thousand and consequently a low note issue, are in great demand. A 1 Rupee note fetched £60 in a Stanley Gibbons Auction recently. The Seychelle Islands are another interesting area for the investor. Early notes of 1919 appear from time to time and are very attractive in design. An emergency issued 50 cts. note of 1919 handsigned by the Island Governor Eustace Hines was sold recently for over £300. Mauritius notes of the 19th Century turn up occasionally. The notes of the 1860s are popular among collectors and are a good investment. The Government issues of the 1920 period are very hard to obtain and the investor should purchase the issues as soon as he possibly can. Any notes issued during King George V's reign are with one or two exceptions rare. Almost invariably 19th Century notes are very rare. This then is the exciting story of the British Empire. As the investor can see the scope is enormous. The surface has only been scratched and the investor can easily make a profitable excursion into this exciting series.

BUYING AT AUCTION

by Richard Ashton

What is an auction? An auction is a sale where goods are offered by the auctioneer acting on behalf of a vendor and assuming that one has followed the correct procedure anyone is free to bid in the sale. True auction sales are held in public; these should be clearly distinguished from postal auctions where bids are only sent by post or phone, and the actual sale held 'in camera' ie not open to the public.

The London auction season commences early in September continuing through the New Year to the end of July. My chairman often comments (tongue in cheek?) 'why the break for one month' but after eleven months of solid 'hammering' everyone involved in auctions including the buyers needs that break to collect their thoughts and possibly their finances! Most of the major auctioneers hold sales twice a month with each sale averaging three days with four or five sessions. Sales are divided into two main categories, general and specialised. Whatever level of collecting or investing you have reached either type of sale can provide treasure trove for the serious buyer.

In a General Sale will be found miscellaneous collections which, when purchased can be sorted so that you retain the stamps or banknotes you require and then re-offer the balance through the auctioneer, possibly with some of your duplicates and therefore recoup some or all of the original purchase price. Also you will find country lots which would form a good basis to start a new section of your collection as well as scarcer singles and sets to fill in gaps in an established collection. Prices range in this type of sale from as little as a few pounds up to many hundreds, or more.

In the field of philately, specialised auctions are often composed of a 'named' collection, that is to say it is being offered on behalf of the collector who has formed the study and who is probably a 'household' name as far as collectors are concerned.

This type of sale covers all fields of philately and may be specialised — Great Britain or more obscure, perhaps Mongolia. Generally, these sales are attended by the more erudite collector or astute investor but it is an excellent idea for the newcomer to attend these sales if only to observe the 'opposition'. Whichever sale you attend remember the auctioneer and his staff are there offering a service which extends to both vendor and buyer so they will be pleased to advise you.

How do I participate at an auction? There are two ways of buying at auction, by post or by bidding personally in the room. When you obtain a catalogue from an auctioneer you will find each lot described and numbered. In addition the auctioneer states his valuation of the lots worth. This valuation is an essential guide to the new buyer. Also you will find a printed bid-form therein which enables you to enter your bids from the comfort of your own home and is imperative if you reside abroad or are unable to attend the sale in person. On this form for 'first-time' buyers there is an area in which to enter a reference which can be your banker or a dealer. If you are successful in any of your bids you will receive an invoice, and upon receipt of your cheque the auctioneer will despatch your purchases.

Before attending a sale in person for the first time it is most important to advise the auctioneer well in advance giving references. The auctioneer then has ample time to take them up prior to the sale. When you arrive at the Auction Rooms you will be asked to fill in a card with your name and address, in return you will be given a numbered bidding card. Numbers are used to ensure complete anonymity to those wishing it. When the lot you are interested in is announced by the auctioneer he will call a starting price. Assuming this is acceptable to you, you should raise your card to indicate a bid. If there is no other bidding then the lot will be knocked down to you at one bid above the auctioneers starting price. Another bidder may mean you have to raise your card again and so on until either party drops out. After the sale you may then collect and make payment for your purchases.

BANKNOTES AROUND THE WORLD

The photographs which follow show some of the most interesting notes from the different countries of the world. All are 'collectors' items' and their value is increasing each year.

John Law, sentenced to death for killing a man, escaped and fled to France where he met the Duke of Orleans in a gambling den. The Duke was so impressed with his mathematical flair that he subsequently hired Law to sort out the nation's finances resulting in Law becoming Comptroller General of France. His early notes of the Banque Generale paid out to a fixed rate of gold. The King had been in the habit of altering the gold rate to suit his needs and the result was that Law's bank became very popular throughout France. Quite worn John Law notes fetch between £100 and £200, the scarcer dates fetch up to £500.

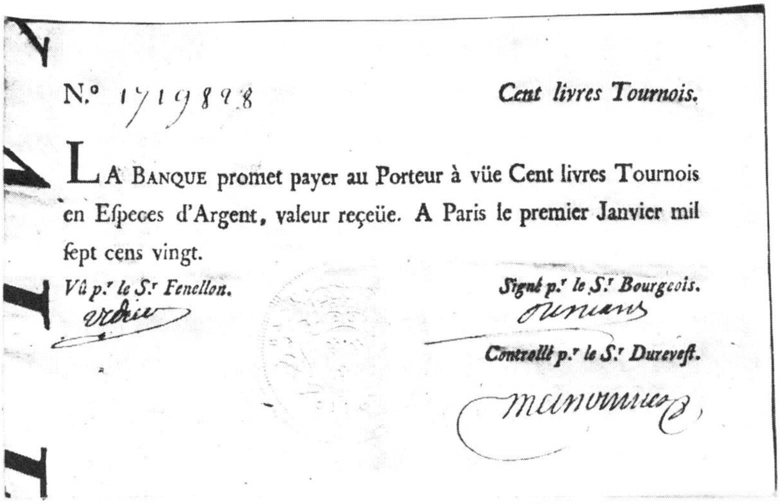

Collecting military currency of World War II has a large following. Great rarities include these Italian notes overprinted with high denominations and in use for one week at the time the italians switched to the Allied side. Allied Military currency replaced them. Only five are known and they have changed hands at £400.

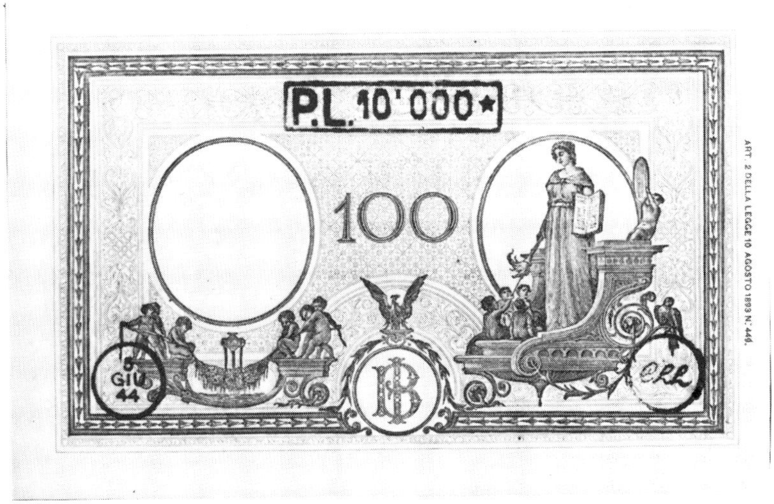

War notes form one of the most popular fields of notaphily and Prisoner of War and Concentration Camp notes are particularly sought after. Notes exist from most of the infamous camps. This one was issued at Buchenwald. Such notes usually fetch about £40 though there are some common issued like Theresienstadt and Litzmanstadt which can often be picked up for a pound or two each.

Ethiopia has produced some magnificent notes showing tigers, elephants and lions. Only recently was it discovered that notes existed for "Bank of Abyssinia" as well as "Ethiopia" yet they are as modern as 1929. This 500 thalers, which would buy a house in its day, is believed to be unique.

Superb engravings which are the hall-mark of Spanish and Portuguese issues aften add to the value. This Portuguese 100 escudos of 1927 is extremely rare and fetches over £400.

South African notes are among the most popular of all issues. This Union of South Africa Gold Certificate represents £10,000 in gold — its face value is prohibitive for most collectors!

his note "type" has been sed for various commonealth countries like olomon Islands, Fiji and alkland Islands. They are all ery rare and seldom get ffered on the open market.

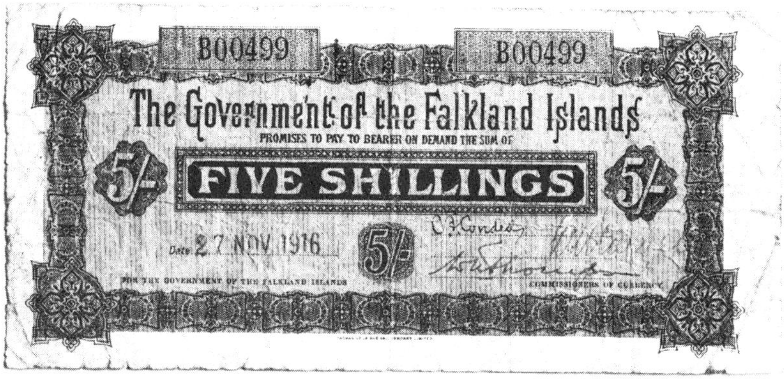

British Banks

It is not always realised that the Bank of England was not the only bank to issue notes in England. At one time more than 900 banks issued their own notes. These are always popular with collectors. They ussually turn up in circulated condition and fetch high prices even so. Rare notes like the 20th century West Yorkshire Bank can fetch £450.

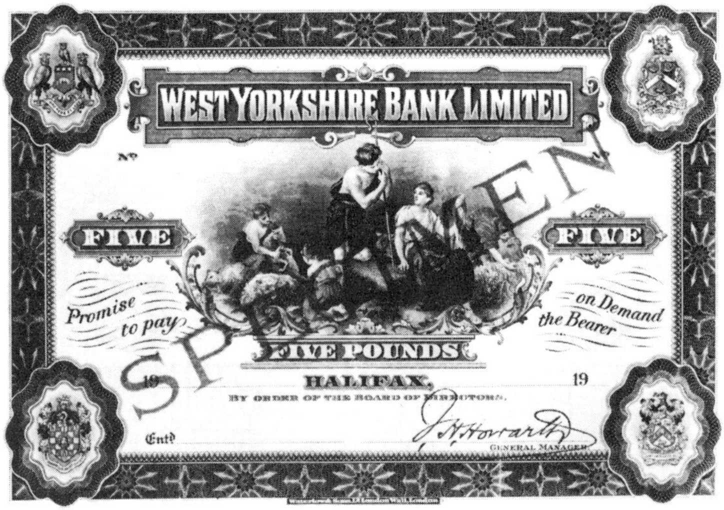

Mafieking Siege Notes

War notes are well collected and the investor can find them lucrative. The Mafeking £1 can be expected to sell for over £200 yet the 10s, of which some 10,000 were printed, can still be obtained for around £35. The £1 depicts the home-made gun 'Wolf' named after Baden Powell 'The wolf that never sleeps.

General Gordon Notes.

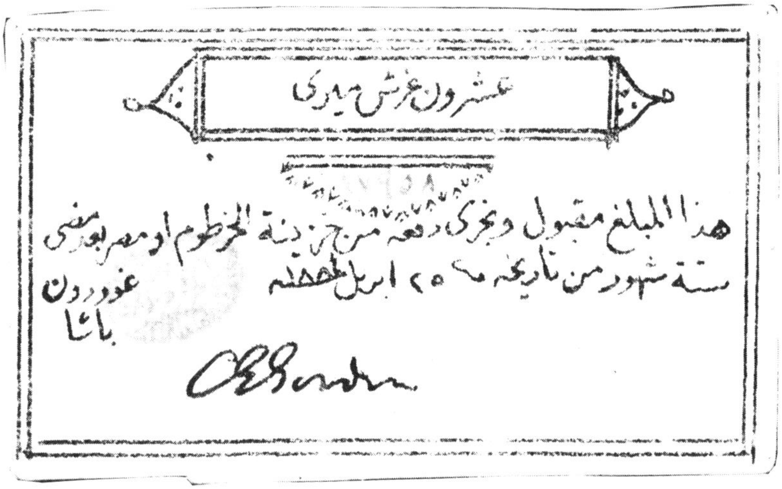

This issue of notes was made shortly before General Gordon was killed. Most of the issues were hand-signed by Gordon, though because this took up important time, heliograph signatures were experimented with but found unsatisfactory. The hand-signature, however, invariably seems to fetch more money at auction which shows the investor that just because an item is rare is not a gurantee that it will fetch more money. A clean card-note of Gordon fetches at least £100, rarer denominations much more — the £50 Egyptian sold in 1974 for $3,000. (only 200 were issued). Heliograph signatures usually fetch £70 to£80. So few of these notes turn up that it is likely their value will increase considerably.

Banknote collecting is well advanced in Germany where early state notes like this one for 10 Thaler Courant issued in 1857, sell for £250.

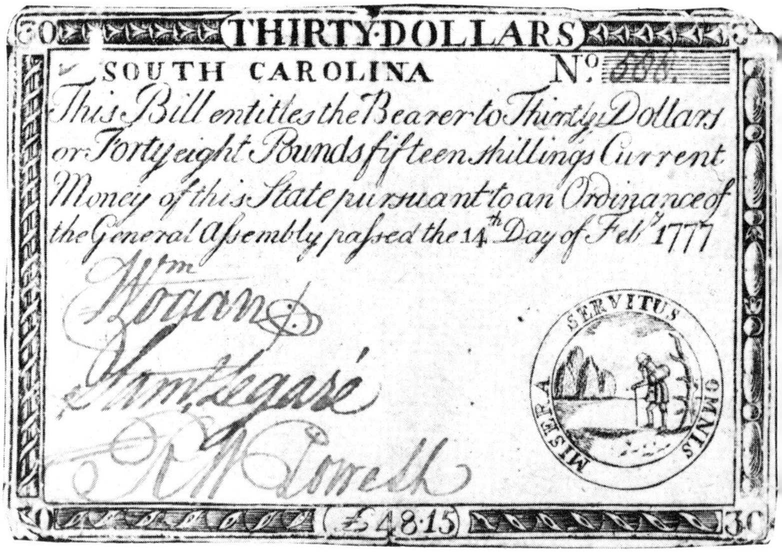

Colonial issues of America at the time of the War of Independence are in great demand, and include notes signed by signatories to the Declaration of Independence. This South Carolina note of 1777 is handsigned by pioneers of America. They range in price from £10 to £1,000.

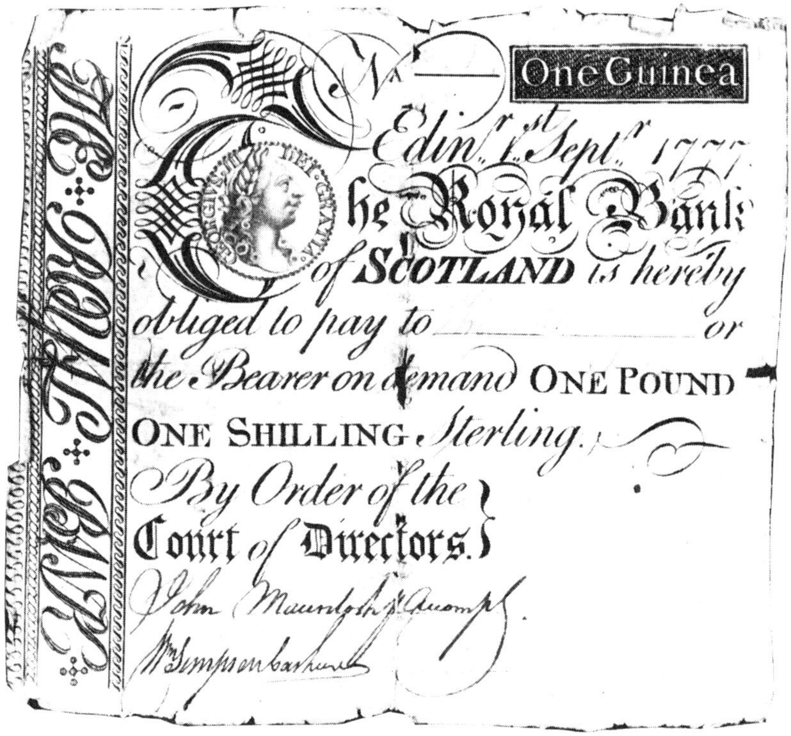

The 'Red Head' note of the Royal Bank of Scotland — one of the first coloured notes in the British Isles.

19TH CENTURY ENGLISH BANKS

The complex history of English Country Banking in the 19th Century has been well documented. Not so has that of the banknotes which were issued. Details are available but perusal of many volumes is necessary in order to extract the type of information useful to collectors. The object of this book then is to provide particulars of the banks known to have issued notes and in additon some basic historical and legal 'background' essential to the collector for a proper appreciation of the many issues. The list of issuing banks is divided into two sections, Joint Stock Banks and Private Banks. These are frequently but erroneously combined in published lists under the heading 'Private Banks', but a joint stock bank ie a bank of which the shares are held by the public is no more 'private' than is, say, Lloyds Bank today. Collectors can distinguish between the two by the manner in which the notes are signed. Those of joint stock banks are normally signed on behalf of the Company by the manager, cashier or other official while notes of private banks are usually signed by or on behalf of the partnership by one or more of the partners.

The Lists have been compiled from official returns and from contemporary records. Only banks known to have issued are included. There were upwards of 700 English country banks at the beginning of the 19th Century and around 500 recorded as having issued notes are listed. Some banks omitted may have in fact issued and should any such notes come to light in the future an extension to the Lists will be necessary. The banking system existing in England in the early 19th Century was vastly different to that which we know today. Apart from the Bank of England which enjoyed considerable Governmental privilege and which reigned supreme in London, the pattern of English banking consisted of numerous small local firms and partnerships which engaged wholly or partly in the business of banking. The issuing of notes was at that time considered to be an integral part of banking and the majority of the small banks did issue. In fact in the closing years of the Napoleonic wars many firms engaged primarily in mining or metallurgy issued their own notes. To that extent they were 'bankers' and where recorded their notes have been included in the Lists.

Outside London there were no banks of any size thanks to legislation which limited the number of partners to six thus precluding the establishment of joint stock banks. There was in consequence no branch system such as we know today, this in marked contrast to the position in Scotland where the absence of legislative interference had resulted in the formation of larger banks with branches throughout the country. In 1837 in Scotland there were 24 banks in all and these had 274 branches. In England there were 351 banks, all independent, and nearly all of which operated from a single office. The two systems had a decisive effect on the circulation of notes.

In England the note issue remained localised. A tradesman in Dorset could not be expected to accept payment freely in notes of a bank in Northumberland the very existence of which was unknown to him. Bank of England notes, not legal tender in these days, did not circulate to any degree far beyond the capital and a radius of thirty miles could be reckoned as their limit. In Scotland a note of, say, the Commercial Bank of Scotland, was as readily acceptable in Aberdeen as it was in Dumfries, the branch system ensuring nationwide recognition of both the bank and its notes. The position in England was further influenced by the prohibition in 1826 of the issue of notes under £5.

Obviously then banknotes could only circulate within the limited area in which the private bank was known and its credit accepted. The many failures of these small firms did nothing to enhance public confidence in paper money. Gold and silver coin with all the inherent inconvenience of transportation was therefore the main medium of currency. Again this fact contrasted with the position in Scotland where notes of the larger banks resulted in paper providing the main circulation and the difficulty and expense of moving large quantities of coin from one part of the country to another was avoided.

Clearly then the circulation of banknotes in England at the beginning of the century was in a state of chaos and pressure was put on the Government to do something about it. In the King's Speech to Parliament in 1826 it was announced that protection was to be afforded to the public by placing on a firmer foundation the currency and circulating credit of the country. A strengthening of the English banking system was obviously the first task but the stumbling block here was the Bank of England or rather the special privileges which it enjoyed. The worst of these privileges was the enactment which prevented any other company or partnership of more than six persons from engaging in banking. Limitation of the number of partners obviously implied limitation in the size and capital of a private bank, and the Government acted by bringing pressure to bear on the Bank of England which eventually consented to the establishment of joint stock banks with no limit to the number of partners (or shareholders). Not until 1833 however were the first English Joint Stock banks fully in operation outside London and the seeds of the present day banking system sown.

The Bank Charter Act of 1844 and Limitation of Note Issues

The history of the note issues of the English country banks is one of continuous legal restrictions resulting finally in their extinction. Some of the restrictions were certainly necessary in view of the many excesses but much could be attributed to the influence of the Bank of England where sights were set for a monopoly of note issue. As stated previously, the size of private banks was restricted by limitation of the number of partners to not more than six. Issue of notes by banks operating within 65 miles of London was also forbidden. In 1826 the Chancellor of the Exchequer proposed to the Bank of England:

1 That the Bank should establish branches in country towns.

2. That the Bank should consent to the establishment of joint stock banks of issue beyond sixty-five miles of London.

The Bank acceded to the first without any difficulty but only with great reluctance consented to the second. Accordingly branches of the Bank of England were opened as follows,

Manchester	September 21st 1826
Birmingham	January 1st 1827
Liverpool	July 2nd 1827
Bristol	July 12th 1827
Leeds	August 23rd 1827
Newcastle	April 21st 1828
Hull	January 2nd 1829
Plymouth	May 1st 1834
Portsmouth	May 16th 1834

Branches also opened at Exeter, Gloucester, Leicester, Norwich and Swansea, but were for various reasons discontinued. Notes were issued by all branches, payable at the town of issue and at London. Those issued at London were only payable there. Bank of England notes were made legal tender when the Charter was renewed in 1833 by an Act which decreed that such notes for any sum about £5 were legal tender in England and Wales. The most important Act of all was the Bank Charter Act of 1844 which regulated the note issue. Its main provisions may be summarised as follows

1 No person other than a banker who was lawfully issuing his own notes on May 6th 1844 should now be permitted to do so.

2 Any banker ceasing to issue through bankruptcy or any other cause would not be allowed to resume.

3 Issue of notes to be limited to the average circulation during 12 weeks preceding April 27th 1844.

4 On amalgamation the authorised issues could be combined providing the total number of partners of the new bank did not exceed six otherwise issue would cease.

The provisions are self-explanatory. The average circulation referred to in paragraph 3 became known as the authorised circulation'. Any bank issuing in excess of this could be heavily fined. In Scotland authorised circulations were established in the following year but there the banks were permitted to issue in excess up to the limit of the security afforded by the total amount of gold coin held, but not so in England.

Mergers and Amalgamations

Although joint stock banks were permitted to commence operations this fact by itself did not effect an immediate cure for all the troubles. Some of these banks were to succumb through economic difficulties and through bad management, but the foundation of the system was much firmer. As the century progressed, increasing mergers and amalgamations provided the country with strong and stable banking institutions. While the banks gained in strength they decreased in number, and by virtue of the provisions of the 1844 Act the number of notes issued also decreased. The following figures illustrate this point.

Banks of Issue at the time of the 1844 Act

207 private banks with authorised issues of	*£5,153,407*
72 joint stock banks do	*3,495,446*
	£8,648,853

(Bank of England notes : £19,992,000)

Banks of Issue in 1877

113 private banks with authorised issues of	*£3,807,992*
54 joint stock banks do	*2,652,993*
	£6,460,985

(Bank of England notes : £27,733,000)

The last English country bank to issue notes was the Wellington Bank of Fox Fowler Co which joined Lloyds Bank Ltd in 1921

Analysis of Lapsed Issues (to year 1875)

	Joint Stock Banks		Private Banks	
Failed or stopped payment	2	£ 48,101	31	£532,581
Closed or dissolved	7	169,589	10	84,741
Issued Bank of England notes			12	194,992
Ceased issue or opened in London	1	442,371	6	82,592
Ceased on amalgamation	8	182,392	26	388,129
	18	£842,453	85	£1,283,035

Numbers of Country Banks in England and Wales

(issuing and non-issuing banks)
1809-1842

1809	755	1819	587	1831	436
1810	783	1821	521	1832	424
1811	741	1822	526	1833	416
1812	739	1823	547	1835	411
1813	761	1824	547	1836	407
1814	733	1825	544	1837	351
1815	649	1826	554	1838	341
1816	643	1827	465	1839	332
1817	585	1828	456	1840	332
1818	576	1829	460	1841	321

from official statistics

Number of Private Notes on which Stamp Duties were Paid

value in £s

	£2-2/- or less	above £2-2/-
1805	3,200,000	1,200,000
1810	3,500,000	1,000,000
1815	2,800,000	700,000
1820	1,600,000	300,000
1825	3,100,000	800,000

figures rounded up.

Geographical Distribution of Note-Issuing Licences

	1808	1815	1822
Bedford	7	6	7
Berkshire	14	17	8
Brecknock	2	3	3
Buckingham	8	3	5
Cambridge	8	6	7
Cardigan	1	—	1
Carmarthen	5	4	3
Carnarvon	1	—	—
Cheshire	8	8	5
Cornwall	36	21	12
Cumberland	9	5	5
Denbigh	5	5	3
Derby	7	8	5
Devon	51	40	34
Dorset	15	11	12
Durham	10	10	7
Essex	13	13	10
Flint	1	2	4
Glamorgan	9	7	10
Gloucester	34	38	25
Hampshire	31	30	24
Hereford	7	7	7
Hertfordshire	14	12	14
Huntingdon	6	5	5
Isle of Anglesey	1	—	—
Kent	30	31	31
Lancashire	4	6	8
Leicester	8	8	10
Lincoln	24	12	11
Merioneth	2	1	2
Middlesex	4	2	2
Monmouth	4	5	5
Montgomery	5	2	2
Norfolk	20	17	16
Northampton	.22	12	11

	1808	1815	1822
Northumberland	7	5	5
Nottingham	16	13	9
Oxford	16	12	12
Pembroke	2	3	1
Radnor	—	—	—
Rutland	3	2	1
Shropshire	22	21	15
Somerset	51	31	28
Stafford	28	22	17
Suffolk	19	19	17
Surrey	17	14	10
Sussex	22	20	16
Warwick	25	23	20
Westmorland	4	3	3
Wiltshire	25	17	16
Worcester	14	13	12
Yorkshire	68	68	56
totals	755	643	552

CATALOGUE

by James Douglas

While the student can search through hundreds of books dealing with banking to find out information on various issues of notes, until Mr James Douglas compiled this catalogue, no concise work existed to give the collector a guide to values and issues.

Mr Douglas is well known for his academic research work into banking history, particularly of Scottish banks, and over many years compiled this list of English banks. It is recognised that the list will not be complete but it is a good start and collectors are invited to write to us with any additional information which could be incorporated in a subsequent edition.

Mr Douglas has recently retired from the service of a Scottish bank and is curator of the Banknote Collection of the Institute of Bankers in Scotland. He is President of the Scottish Numismatic Society and a Past President of the Scottish Philatelic Society. His research in the field of Scottish Postal History is reflected in several of the Scottish Postmark Group Handbooks which have gained major awards in a number of international exhibitions.

C C Narbeth, Managing Director, Stanley Gibbons Currency Ltd.

It is difficult to give accurate valuations for English Joint Stock and Private Banks. This is because, despite the accuracy of the statistics produced in this book, the surviving notes are not always proportionate. It can happen that a bank with a very small circulation has nevertheless left behind a large number of notes, and a bank with a large circulation has in fact destroyed most of its notes leaving very few for collectors. It has therefore been felt best to give a general guide to value.

It will be found that 90 per cent of the banknotes are rare, but, being a less developed hobby than philately, their prices in comparison are ludicrously low.

Including varieties of design, branch issues and different denominations it is theoretically possible to build up a collection of around 5,000 notes. But few collections exist at the moment with much more than 500 different notes in them and 'new finds' are continually turning up.

Collectors will be pleased to know that there are a great many books on individual banks and banking history from which much information can be gleaned.

Even a small collection of a few dozen notes can tell a fascinating part of British history and will give great pleasure to the owner. The stories behind failures and bankruptcies, some involving criminal proceedings and prison sentences, can be quite extraordinary.

Generally it will be found that the notes in this catalogue sell on average between £12 and £30, though these prices cannot be expected to remain in this bracket as more collectors join the hobby.

PRIVATE BANKS by James Douglas

Bank or location	Firm or partnership	Founded	Issue ceased	Authorised circ.	Present connection
Abergavenny	Crawshay Bailie & Co	1837	1867		
Abernant Ironworks	Tapperden & Co				
Aberystwyth	Benson & Co	1815	1836		
Aberystwyth Bank Banc Y Llong	Evans Jones & Davies	1762	1815		Midland
Abingdon	Child & Co	1800	1816		
Abingdon Bank Abingdon & Wantage Bank	Knapp & Co	1801	1848	29316	
Andover Bank	Gilbert & Co. Heath & Co.	1790	1861	17751	Lloyds
Ashbourne	Bradley & Co.	1829	1838		
Arundel	Bushby & Co.	1790	1814		
Ashburton	Abraham & Co.	1800	1812		
Ashford Bank	Jemmett & Co. Pomfret Burra & Co.	1790	1902	11849	Lloyds
Ashton-under-Lyne	Sikes & Hide	1800			
Atherstone Old Bank	Wm Hanson & Co	1790	1801		
Aylesbury Old Bank	W Rickford & Son Rickford & Hume T R Cobb & Co. Cobb Bartlett & Co.	1795	1902	48461	Lloyds
Aylsham Bank	T R & G Copeman	1809	1855		
Baldock Bank Baldock & Biggleswade Bank	Wells Hogge & Co. C & W Hogge	1807	1893	37223	Lloyds
Banbury Bank	Gillett & Towney	1784	1918	43457	Barclays
Banbury Old Bank	Cobb Wheatley & Cobb R & E Cobb Cobb & Son T R Cobb & Sons	1783	1902	55153	Lloyds

Bank or location	Firm or partnership	Founded	Issue ceased	Authorised circ.	Present connection
Banbury New Bank	Bignell Haydon & Wyatt Heydon & Co.	1784	1800		
Bank in Newcastle see Newcastle Davidson Bland & Co.	Lambton & Co.				
Bank of Wantage see Farrington Bank					
Barnsley	Beckett Birks & Co. Beckett Clarke & Co.	1800	1840		
Barnstaple Bank	Cunliffe Roch & Gribble Drake Gribble & Co. Marshall & Co. Marshall & Harding	1791	1887	17182	Lloyds
Basingstoke & Odiham Bank	Cole Seymour & Co	1806	1864	24730	Lloyds
Bath	Euclid Shaw & Co.	1808	1810		
Bath Old Bank	Clement Tugwell & Mackenzie	1780	1891		Nat. West
Bath City Bank	George Moger & Son	1819	1856	4572	Nat. West
Bedford Bank	Thomas Barnard & Co.	1799	1915	34218	Nat. West
Bedford & Bed- fordshire Bank	Trapp Halfhead & Co.	1828	1849	8515	
Bedford & Leighton Buzzard Bank	Bassett & Co. Bassett Son & Harris	1812	1896	36829	Barclays
Berwick Bank	Mowbray & Co.	1803	1815		
Berwick Bank see Exchange Bank, Newcastle	Surtees Burdon & Brandling	1775	1803		
Beverley	Bower Hall & Co.	1790	1875		
Beverley Bank see Hull Old Bank	Pease & Liddell				
Bewdley Bank	Nichols Baker & Crane	1782	1862	18597	Midland
Bicester & Oxford- shire Bank	Wooton Tubb & Co. G & H Tubb	1793	1920	27090	Barclays
Bideford	Thomas Burnard	1810	1825		
Bideford Bank	Ley & Co.	1790	1843		Nat. West
Bilston Bank	Geo Rushbery & Co. William Jones & Son.	1824	1864		Midland

Bank or location	Firm or partnership	Founded	Issue ceased	Authorised circ.	Present connection
Birmingham	Taylor & Lloyds Lloyds & Co.	1765	1865	38816	Lloyds
Birmingham	Attwoods Spooner & Co	1791	1865	23695	Lloyds
Birmingham	Gibbins & Lovell	1825	1829		
Birmingham and Warwickshire Bank	Moilliet & Sons	1766	1857	18132	Lloyds
Bishops Stortford Bank see Essex Bank					
Bishop Waltham	Gunner & Co	1809	1845		
Blackburn	Cunliffe Brooks & Co.	1792	1840		Lloyds
Blandford Bank	Bastard & Oak Oak & Snow	1787	1858	9723	
Bognor Bank	G J Call & Co.		1826		
Bolton le Moors	Hardcastle Ormerod & Co	1818	1878		
Borough Bank of Sheffield		1839	1841		
Boston Bank	Garfit Claypon & Co.	1754	1889	75069	Lloyds
Boston Bank	Gee & Co.	1788	1874	15161	Midland
Boston	Ingleton & Co. Barnards & Co.	1790	1814		
Bowling Ironworks (nr. Bradford)					
Bradford Old Bank	H A & W M Harris & Co. Pickover Harris & Co.	1803	1864	12676	Barclays
Bradley Ironworks	Wilkinson & Co.				
Braintree Bank	Crowe James & Co.	1801	1807		
Brecon Bank see Chepstowe Old Bk.	Bromage Snead & Co.				
Brecon Old Bank	Wilkins & Co.	1778	1890	68271	Lloyds
Bridgnorth Bank	Coopers & Purton	1817	1840		Midland
Bridgnorth & Brosley Bank Brosley & Bridgnorth Bank	Vickers Son & Pritchard Pritchards & Boycott Pritchards Gordon & Co.	1800	1888	26717	Lloyds
Bridport Bank	Gundry & Co.	1790	1847	24698	

Bank or location	Firm or partnership	Founded	Issue ceased	Authorised circ.	Present connection
Bridgwater Bank	E & J Sealy Sealy & Prior	1790	1874	10028	Lloyds
Brighton Bank	Widney & Co.	1800	1842		
Brighton Old Bank	Mitchell Mills & Co.	1790	1826		
Brighton Union Bank	Hall West & Borrer	1805	1887	33794	Barclays
Brighthelmston Bank					
Bristol Bank	Miles Hereford & Co.	1760	1877	48277	
Bristol Bullion Bank	Browne Cavenagh & Browne	1811	1825		
Bristol City Bank	Ireland Bengough & Co.	1794	1834		
Bristol Old Bank	Baillie Ames & Co	1750	1844		Nat West
Bristol Tolzey Bank	Warrall & Co.	1782	1819		
Brixham Bank	Hine Holdsworth & Pomeroy	1810	1824		
Bromsgrove Bank	Rufford & Co. Rufford Biggs & Co.	1792	1851	16799	
Brosley & Bridgnorth Bank — see Bridgnorth & Brosley					
Brymbo Ironworks	Wilkinson & Co.				
Buckingham Bank	Bartlett Parrott & Hern Bartlett & Co.	1779	1902	29657	
Burlington & Driffield Bank	Harding Mortlock & Co.	1802	1882	12745	Midland
Burton	Clay & Co.	1809	1839		
Buxton	Goodwins & Co.	1808	1816		
Bury St. Edmonds Bank	J Worledge & Co. Worledge Huddleston & Co	1844	1880	3201	Barclays
Bury & Suffolk Bank Sudbury Bank Market Bank	Oakes Bevan & Co James Oakes & Son	1795	1897	82362	Lloyds
Caerleon	Fothergill & Co.	1810			
Calne	Croudy & Co.	1806	1809		
Cambridge	Mortlock & Co	1754	1889	25744	Barclays
Cambridge Bank	Fisher & Son	1790	1845		

Bank or location	Firm or partnership	Founded	Issue ceased	Authorised circ.	Present connection
Cambridge & Cambridgeshire Bank	Foster & Foster	1817	1904	49916	Lloyds
Canterbury Bank	Hammond & Co Gipps Simmons & Gipps	1788	1903	33671	Lloyds
Canterbury Union Bank	Halford Baldock & Co.	1790	1841		
Carmarthen Bank	Waters & Jones	1800	1832		
Castle Bank, Bristol	Rickett Thorne & Co.	1810	1826		
Cardiff	Guest & Co.	1810			
Cardiff	Towgood & Co	1819	1855	7001	Lloyds
Carlisle	J M Head & Co	1804	1840		Midland
Carlisle Old Bank	Thos. Forster & John Forster	1790	1830		
Carmarthen Bank	Morris & Sons		1871	23597	Nat West
Chatham	Budgon & Co.	1811	1816		
Chatham & Sheerness Bank	Dann Bentham & Co	1800	1805		
Chelmsford	Crickett Menish & Co.	1792	1825		
Cheltenham & Winchcombe Bank	Fisher & Ashmore	1797	1819		
Chepstowe Old Bank Chepstowe Bank Monmouth Old Bank Monmouth Bank Brecon Bank Ross & Hereford Bank	Bromage Snead & Co Snead & Co	1819	1866	9387	
Chertsey Bank	T & G La Costa La Coste & Sons	1808	1867	3436	Barclays
Chester Old Bank	Williams & Co.	1792	1847		
Chesterfield	Coller & Co.	1808	1826		
Chesterfield	Gillett & Co.	1790	1825		
Chichester Bank Chichester Old Bank	Ridge & Co	1783	1841		
Chipping Norton Bank	Corgan Paget & Matthews	1790	1816		
Christchurch Bank	Tice & Welch	1837	1849	2849	Lloyds

Bank or location	Firm or partnership	Founded	Issue ceased	Authorised circ.	Present connection
Christchurch Wimborne & Ringwood Bank	Dean & Co	1800	1825		
City Bank, Exeter	Milford & Co. Milford Snow & Co.	1786	1901	21527	Nat West
Colchester	Twinning & Mills	1760			
Colchester	Crickett & Co.	1774	1790		
Colchester Bank	Round Green & Co. Gurney Round Green & Co.	1774	1896	25082	Barclays
Colchester & Essex Bank Hadleigh Bank Witham & Essex Bank	Mills & Co.		1891	48704	
Collumpton & Devonshire Bank	Chambers Granger & Co.	1809	1812		
Commercial Bank, Newcastle	Foster & Co.	1784			
Commercial Bank, Stockton	Skinner & Co	1815	1836		Nat West
Commercial Bank, Stokesley	Thomas Simpson & Co.	1796	1802		
Copper Miners Bank see Miners' Bank	Owen Williams & Co				
Copper Smelting Works Swansea	Owen Williams & Co				
Cornish Bank, Truro	Tweedy Williams & Co	1771	1879	49868	Lloyds
Coventry Bank	Little & Woodcock	1762	1865	12045	Midland
Cowes	Day & Co	1800	1804		
Craven Bank	Birkbeck & Co. Birkbecks Alcock & Co.	1791	1884	77154	
Darlington	John Clement	1772	1785		
Darlington Bank Durham Bank Stockton-onTees Bank Sunderland Bank	Jonathan Backhouse & Co.	1774	1896	86218	Barclays
Dartford	Budgon & Co.	1807	1826		
Darlington Bank	Baxter & Co.	1817	1826		
Derby Bank	W & S Evans & Co.	1771	1877	13332	Nat West
Derby Bank	Samuel Smith & Co.	1806	1902	41304	Nat West

Bank or location	Firm or partnership	Founded	Issue ceased	Authorised circ.	Present connection
Derby Old Bank	Crompton Newton & Co.		1877	27237	
Devizes & Wiltshire Bank	Hughes Locke Oliver & Co Locke & Co. Locke Tugwell & Meek	1803	1883	20674	Lloyds
Devon County Bank, Exeter	Cole Holroyd & Co.	1807	1842		Nat West
Devonport Bank Plymouth Dock Bank	Hodge & Norman	1804	1889	10664	Barclays
Diss Bank Diss & Harling Bank	Oakes Fincham & Co.	1802	1871	10657	
Doncaster Bank	Leatham Tew & Co.	1801	1906	13881	Barclays
Doncaster & Retford Bank	Cooke & Co Beckett & Co.	1801			Nat West
Dorchester Old Bank	Williams & Co. Williams Thornton Sykes & Co.	1786	1897	48807	Lloyds
Dover Old Bank	Fector & Co.	1760	1841		
Dover Union Bank	Latham & Co.	1789	1846		
Dowlais Ironworks Glamorgan	W Taitt & W Lewis	1818	1830		
Dudley Old Bank	Dixon Dalton & Co.	1790	1843		
Durham Bank see Darlington Bank					
Durham Bank	Hopper & Co	1787	1802		
Durham Bank	Richardson & Co.	1778	1815		
East Cornwall Bank	Robins Foster & Co.	1807	1887	112280	Barclays
East Riding Bank, Beverley	Bower Hutton & Co.	1790	1920	53392	Nat West
Essex Bank — Bishop Stortford Bank	Sparrow & Co Sparrow Tufnell & Co.	1805	1893	69637	Barclays
Exchange Bank, Newcastle	Surtees & Burdon	1768	1803		
Exeter Bank	Sanders & Co.	1769	1901	37804	Nat West
Exeter City Bank see City Bank, Exeter	Milford & Co.				
Fakenham Bank	Gurney & Co. Gurneys Birkbeck & Co.	1792		24293	Barclays

Bank or location	Firm or partnership	Founded	Issue ceased	Authorised circ.	Present connection
Falmouth	G C Fox & Sons	1808	1810		
Farnham Bank	Knight & Co James Knight & Sons Stevens & Co.	1793	1886	14202	Lloyds
Farnham Old Bank	Cock & Lamport	1793	1817		
Farringdon Bank Bank of Wantage	Barnes Medley & Ansell	1806	1861	8977	
Faversham Bank	Bax Jones & Co. Hilton Rigden & Rigden	1796	1902	6681	Nat West
Fleet Bank	(Issue suppressed)				
Fordingbridge Bank	Kelleway & Co.	1808	1816		
Gainsborough Bank	W Hornby & J Esdaile Gillet & Co	1790	1812		
Glastonbury & Shepton Mallet Bank					
Glamorgan	Macworth & Co.	1790			
Gloucester Old Bank	Russel & Skey	1782	1832		Lloyds
Godalming Bank	Mellersh & Keen Mellersh & Co.	1808	1893	6322	Lloyds
Gosport	Richard Bingham		1821		
Grantham Bank	Hardy & Co.	1819	1895	30372	Midland
Grantham Bank	Kewney & King	1812	1848	19401	
Guildford	Haydon & Smallpiece	1765	1883	14524	Lloyds
Hadleigh Suffolk Bank see Ipswick & Needham Market Bank	Mills Bawtree & Co.				
Halesworth Bank Halesworth & Suffolk Bk.	Gurneys Turner & Co Gurneys Birkbeck & Co.	1782	1896		Barclays
Harwich	Cox Cobbold & Co.	1807	1893	5778	Lloyds
Hastings Old Bank	Hawkhurst Smith & Co Smith Hilder & Co	1791	1857	38038	
Hastings & Halisham Bank	Breeds Francomb & Co.	1806	1826		
Haverfordwest	W & F Fortune	1801	1808		
Helston Union Bank	Vivian Grylls & Co.	1788	1879		
Hemel Hempstead	Smith & Wittingstall	1811	1856	23842	

Bank or location	Firm or partnership	Founded	Issue ceased	Authorised circ.	Present connection
Hereford City & County Bk.	Bodenham Garrett & Son F H Matthews & Co.	1827	1863	22364	
Hereford Ross & Archenfield Bk.	Morgan & Adam	1820	1863	27625	
Hertfordshire Hitchen Bk. see Hitchen Hereford & Luton Bank					
Hertford Bank	Christie & Cathrow	1807	1816		
Hertford & Ware Bank	S Adams & Co.	1813	1856	23635	
Hexham	William Bell Blake Reed & Co.	1821	1839		
Hitchin Hereford & Luton Bank	Sharples & Co. Sharples, Tuke, Lucas & Seebohm.	1827	1890	38764	Barclays
Holywell	Douglas & Smalley	1822	1839		Midland
Honiton Bank	Flood & Co.	1786	1847	19015	
Huddersfield Old Bank	John Dodson & Son	1800	1825		
Hull	T R Raikes & Co.	1790	1861		
Hull & Kingston on Hull Bank	Smith Bros & Co.	1784	1902	19979	Nat West
Hull Old Bank Beverley Bank	Pease & Liddell Peases Hoare & Pease	1754	1893	48807	Barclays
Huntingdon Town & County Bank	Rust & Veaseys Veasey Desborough & Co.	1804	1896	56501	Barclays
Ipswich Bank	Bacon Cobbold & Co. Crickett Truelove & Co.	1786	1904	21901	Lloyds
Ipswich & Needham Market Bank Manningtree & Mistley Bank	Alexander & Co. Gurneys Alexander Birkbeck & Co.	1745	1896	80609	Barclays
Kendal Bank	Wakefield Crewdson & Co.	1788	1893	44663	Barclays
Kentish Bank (Maidstone)	Springet & Penfold Mercer Randall & Co. Wigan Mercer & Co. Brenchley Stacey & Co.	1818	1888	19895	Nat West
Kettering	John C Gotch & Sons	1792	1857	9192	
Kidderminster Old Bank	Farley Turner & Jones	1793	1856		
Kingsbridge Bank	Nicholson & Co.	1829	1832		Lloyds

Bank or location	Firm or partnership	Founded	Issue ceased	Authorised circ.	Present connection
Kington & Radnorshire Bank	Davies Crummer & Oliver	1808	1910	26050	Midland
Kirkby Stephen & Westmoreland Bank					
Knighton Bank	Davies & Co	1808	1856	9090	Midland
Knaresborough Old Bank	Torry & Harrison Harrison & Co	1785	1875	21825	Barclays
Lampeter Bank	Jones Evans & Co	1831	1839	8290	Lloyds
Lane End Staffordshire Bk Langton Staffordshire Bk	C. Harvey & Son	1837	1866	5624	
Latterworth Bank		1814			
Launceston	Harvey & Sons	1811	1825		
Ledbury Bank	Hankins & Co. Webb & Son	1790	1815		Lloyds
Leek & Staffordshire Bk Leek & Congleton Bank	Fowler Gaunt & Co	1825	1847	4009	Lloyds
Leeds Bank Leeds Old Bank	Beckett & Co	1750	1920	53357	Nat West
Leeds Union Bank	W Williams Brown & Co	1812	1900	37459	Lloyds
Leicester	Bentley & Buxton	1783	1803		
Leicester Bank	Pagets & Co.	1825	1895	32322	Lloyds
Leominster	Coleman Morris & Sons	1790	1826		
Leominster	Woodhouse & Co.	1827	1832		
Lewes Bank	Wood Hall & Co	1805	1825		
Lewes Old Bank	Hurley Molineux & Co. Molineux & Co.	1789	1887	44836	Barclays
Lichfield Bank	Barker & Co. Palmer & Greene	1765	1855		
Lincoln Bank	Smith & Co. Smith Ellison & Co.	1775	1902	100342	Nat West
Lincolnshire Bank Lyme Regis Lincolnshire Bank	Gurney & Co.	1782	1888	42817	Barclays
Llandovery Bank & Llandilo Bank	David Jones & Co	1800	1909	25592	Lloyds
Llanedloes Bank	William Herbert & Co.		1816		

Bank or location	Firm or partnership	Founded	Issue ceased	Authorised circ.	Present connection
Liverpool	Leyland Bullins & Co.	1807	1840		Midland
Looe	Jonathan Binns & Sons		1819		
Loughborough Bank	Middleton & Craddock	1790	1878	7359	Midland
Longton Staffordshire Bank see Lane End Staffordshire Bank					
Ludlow	Coleman & Wellings	1800	1826		
Ludlow Bank Ludlow & Tenbury Bank		1840	1864		Lloyds
Ludlow & Bishop Castle Bank		1800	1820		
Luton	Hampson & Austin	1806	1824		
Lyme Regis & Lincoln shire Bank — see Lincolnshire Bank	Gurney & Co				
Lyme Regis & Norfolk Bank	Jarvis & Jarvis	1808	1888	13917	Barclays
Lymington Bank	C & S St. Barbe St. Barbe & Co.	1788	1896	5038	Lloyds
Macclesfield	Daintry & Ryle	1810	1841		
Macclesfield Bank	Brockhurst & Co.	1816	1891	15760	Nat West
Maidstone Bank	Sir W Bishop & Co.	1805	1816		
Malton Whitby & Scarborough Bank	Hayes & Co.	1792	1814		
Manchester	Thomas Crewdson	1824	1826		
Mansfield & Chesterfield Bank	Robinson & Broadhurst	1804	1840		
Manningtree Bank Manningtree & Colchester Bank	Nunn & Co.	1810	1870	7692	
Manningtree & Mistley Bank — see Ipswich & Needham Market Bank	Alexander & Co				
Margate Bank	Cobb & Co.	1785	1824		Lloyds
Market Drayton	Jervis & Co.	1800	1830		
Marlborough Bank	Tanner & Co.	1793	1858	19073	

Bank or location	Firm or partnership	Founded	Issue ceased	Authorised circ.	Present connection
Marlborough & North Wiltshire New Bank	Ward & Co. Ward Brown & Co.	1803	1850	12490	Lloyds
Marshfield & Gloucestershire Bank	Isaac Baldwin & Co.	1800	1826		
Melksham	Awdry Long & Co. Audrey Long & Co. Freeman & Co.	1792			
	Moule & Co.	1792	1835		Lloyds
Mells Ironworks (Somerset)	James Tussell & Son				
Merionethshire Bank	Jones & Williams Williams & Son	1803	1873	10906	Midland
Milverton	Thomas Young & Co.	1800	1814		
Milverton & Taunton Bk					
Miners Bank (Truro) Copper Miners Bank	Willyams Hodge & Co.	1771	1889	18688	Barclays
Mold	S & J Knight	1823	1831		
Monmouth Old Bank	Bromage & Co.	1819	1894	16385	Lloyds
Monmouthshire Agricultural & Commercial Bank	Bailey, Bailey, Gretix & Williams Bailey & Co.	1784	1868	29335	Nat West
Monmouthshire Newport Old Bank — see Newport Old Bank					
Mount's Bay Commercial Bank	Bolitho Sons & Co.	1807	1889		
Nantwich Bank Nantwich Old Bank	Hewitt Bowman & Co.		1816		
Naval Bank (Plymouth)	Harris Bulteel & Co.	1774	1914	27321	Lloyds
Newark Bank	Godfrey Hutton & Co. Samuel Smith & Co.	1688	1902	28788	Nat West
Newark & Sleaford Bank	Handley Peacock & Co. Peacock Wilson & Co.	1792	1912	51615	
Newbury	Fuller & Graham	1813	1821		
Newbury Bank	Bunny & Slocock Slocock & Co.	1790	1895	36787	Lloyds
Newcastle	Davison Bland & Co Lampton & Co	1788	1908		Lloyds

Bank or location	Firm or partnership	Founded	Issue ceased	Authorised circ.	Present connection
Newcastle	Warwick Lamb Wright & Co				
Newcastle-on-Tyne Old Bank	Bell Cookson Carr & Co Sir W.M. Ridley & Co	1755	1839		
Newmarket Bank	Eaton Hammond & Co.	1799	1905	25098	Barclays
Newmarket Commercial Bank	Bryant & Son	1809	1844		
Newport	Bassett & Co.	1790	1842		Nat West
Newport	Homfray & Co.	1810			
Newport Old Bank Monmouthshire Newport Old Bank	Williams & Son	1826	1851	8600	
New Sarum Bank Salisbury Old Bank	Hetley Everett & Co. Pinckney Bros.	1811	1897	15659	Lloyds
Newton Bank (Newton Abbot)	Wise Farwell Baker & Co.	1817	1841		
Norfolk & Suffolk Bank	Taylor & Dyson	1802		4551	
North Lincolnshire Bank					
North Riding Bank	Hagues & Strickland	1816	1825		
North Riding Bank	Hammond Hirst & Close	1804	1820		
North Riding Bank (Northallerton)	Peirse & Co.	1793	1803		
North & South Shields Bk	Chapman & Co.	1818	1836		
Northumberland Bank (Newcastle)	Batson Wakefield & Scott	1800	1821		
Northwich	Worthington & Co.	1801	1808		
Norwich Crown Bank	Harveys & Co. Harveys & Hudsons	1790	1870	45120	
Norwich & Norfolk Bank	Gurneys & Co. Birkbeck Barclay & Buxton	1790	1896	75372	Barclays
Norwich & Swaffham Bk	Henry Day & Co.	1790	1825		
Nottingham Bank	Samuel Smith & Co.	1688	1902	31047	Nat West
Nottingham Bank Nottingham & Nottinghamshire Bank	Hart Fellows & Co.	1808	1865	10866	Lloyds
Nuneaton Bank	Craddock & Co. Craddock & Bell	1815	1861	5898	Midland

Bank or location	Firm or partnership	Founded	Issue ceased	Authorised circ.	Present connection
Oakhampton	Hawkes & Burd	1807	1816		
Oakhampton	Cann Williams & Co.	1817	1820		
Oswestry Bank	Croxon Jones & Co.	1792	1889	18471	Midland
Oxford	J & R Morrell	1793	1851	14277	
Oxford Old Bank	Herbert Parsons & Co. Parsons Thomson & Co.	1771	1900	34391	Barclays
Oxford University & City Bank	John Lock & Co.	1797	1825		
Oxfordshire Witney Bank	Gillet & Co. John Clinch & Co.	1796	1918	11852	Barclays
Pares Bank (Leicester)		1800			
Peases Old Bank see Hull Old Bank					
Pembrokeshire Bank (Haverfordwest)	John & William Walters	1827	1872	12910	Barclays
Penzance	Batten & Co. Batten Carne & Carne	1795	1890	11405	Barclays
Penzance Union Bank	Ricketts & Co. Boase & Co.	1810	1847	31461	
Penydarran Ironworks (Glamorgan)	Thos. Homfray & W. Forman				
Peterborough	Daniel Yorke & Co.	1802	1862	12545	
Peterborough Bank	Simpson White & Co.	1821	1849	12832	Barclays
Peterborough Bank	Cole Hardy & Co.	1809	1817		
Petersfield Bank	Butterfield & Co.	1833	1844		
Petworth Bank	John Stoveld	1806	1845		
Plymouth Dock Bank see Devonport Bank	Glencross Hodge & Co.				
Pontefract Bank branch of Doncaster Bank	Leatham Tew & Co.				
Portsea	Thomas Wilday	1821	1836		
Ramsgate Old Bank	Austin & Sons	1800	1840		
Reading	J & C Simmonds & Co.	1814	1913	37519	Barclays
Reading Bank	Stephens Blandy & Co. Micklem Stephens & Co.	1790	1899	43271	Lloyds

Bank or location	Firm or partnership	Founded	Issue ceased	Authorised circ.	Present connection
Ramsgate	Burgess Canham & Co.	1808	1864		
Reigate & Barking Bank	Nash & Co. Nash & Neale	1808	1850	13700	
Retford Bank					
Rhayder Bank					
Richmond Bank (Yorkshire)	Gilbert Stapleton & Co. Roper & Priestmen	1792	1902	6889	Barclays
Richmond & Swale-dale Bank	Hutton & Co.	1803	1836		Barclays
Rigwood & Poole Bank Town & County of Poole Bank	Ledgard & Sons	1821	1861	11856	
Ripon	Britain & Co.	1801	1835		
Ripon Bank	Harrison & Co.	1785	1875		
Rochdale	Fentons & Roby Royds & Co.	1819	1867	5590	
Rochdale	Clements & Co	1819	1882		
Rochdale	Rawsons & Co.	1807	1836		
Rochester Chatham & Stroud Bank	Day & Nicholson	1782	1864	10480	
Rochford	Harvey Sons & Co.	1809	1815		
Romsey & Hampton Bank	Wm Fortner & Son Warner Newman & Fortner	1807	1846	3875	Lloyds
Ross Old Bank	Pritchards & Alloway Alloway & MacDougall	1807	1863	4420	Lloyds
Ross & Archenfield Bank	Morgan & Hoskins Morgan & Adams	1820	1863		
Ross & Hereford Bk see Chepstowe Old Bank	Bromage Snead & Co.				
Royds Iron Works					
Royston Bank	J.G. Fordham & Sons Fordham Gibson & Co	1808	1896	16393	Barclays
Rugby	Butlin & Son	1791	1868	17250	Lloyds
Rye Bank (Sussex)	R Curteis Pomfret & Co. Curteis & Co.	1808	1892	29864	Lloyds
Rye Bank (Tendterden)	Pix Billingham & Pix				

Bank or location	Firm or partnership	Founded	Issue ceased	Authorised circ.	Present connection
St. Albans	J S Storey	1804	1848	3743	
St. Albans & Herts Bk	Gibson & Sturt	1845	1847	2333	
St. Ives	James Halse	1808	1813		
Saffron Walden Bank	Gibson Tuke & Gibson	1800	1896	47646	Barclays
Salisbury Salisbury & Fordingham Bk.	Brodie & Co.	1811	1847	23335	
Salisbury City Bank	Burrough & Read	1797	1810		
Salisbury Old Bank see New Sarum Bank	Pinkney Bros.				
Salop Bank	Burton Lloyd & Co.	1808	1892	22338	
Salop Old Bank	Eyton Burton & Co.	1792	1884	65529	Nat West
Sandwich	Emmerson & Co.	1800	1841		
Scarborough Bank Scarborough Old Bank	Woodall Hebden & Co.	1788	1896	24873	Barclays
Scarborough	Lister & Co.	1805	1822		
Selby	Green Myers & Co.	1818	1820		
Shaftesbury Bank Shaftesbury & Hendon Bk	Brodie & King	1834	1847	9813	
Sheerness Bank	Chalk & Co.	1812	1819		
Sherbourne & Dorset Bank	Peter Pew & Co. Pretor & Co.	1740	1843		Nat West
Shields & Sunderland Bank	Cook Robinson & Co.	1803	1816		
Shifnal	Botfield & Co	1808	1824		
Shrewsbury	J Bishop	1802	1806		
Shrewsbury Old Bank	Renton Walker & Miller Rock Eyton & Co. Eyton Reynolds & Bishop	1792	1884	43191	Lloyds
Shrewsbury & Market Drayton Bank	Adams & Co. Adams & Warren	1840	1847	9700	
Shrewsbury & Welshpool Bank	Beck & Co.	1800	1880	25336	Lloyds
Sittingbourne & Milton Bank	Vallance & Sons Vallance & Payne	1824	1888	4789	Lloyds
Skipton Craven Bank					

Bank or location	Firm or partnership	Founded	Issue ceased	Authorised circ.	Present connection
Sleaford Bank	Peacock & Co. Peacock Handley & Kirton	1792	1840		Lloyds
Southampton & Hampshire Bank	Atherley Fall & Co.	1770	1869	6770	Lloyds
Southampton Town & County Bank	Maddison & Pearce	1790	1888	18589	Lloyds
Southwell Bank	Wylde & Co.	1806	1874	14744	
Stafford Old Bank	Stevenson Salt & Co. John Stevenson	1737	1866	14166	Lloyds
Staines	Coggan Morris & Co.	1810	1813		
Staines Bank	Thomas Ashby & Co.	1804	1840		Barclays
Stamford	Collier & Clifford	1807	1812		
Stamford & Rutland Bk	Eaton Cayley & Co.	1800	1891	31858	Barclays
Stanley Colliery (nr Bewdley)	Wm Hughes & J Gretton				
Stockport	Burys Roth & Co.	1800	1803		
Stockton & Cleveland Bk	Lumley Brown & Smith	1774	1815		
Stone Bank (Stoke on Trent)	W Moore	1800	1858	9154	Nat West
Stoney Stratford Bank	Olivers & Co. Bartlett & Co.	1843	1845		Lloyds
Stourbridge	W B Collin	1762	1770		
Stourbridge Old Bank	Bate & Robbins	1770	1851	17560	Midland
Stourbridge Bank	Ruffords & Wragge Rufford & Co.	1792	1851	17295	
Stowmarket Bank	Oakes Bevan & Co.	1805	1900		
Stratford on Avon	Battersbee & Morris	1790	1815		
Stratford on Avon	Whitehead & Co.				
Sudbury Bank see Bury & Suffolk Bk.	Oakes Bevan & Co.				
Sunderland	Russell Wilson & Wade	1787	1802		
Sunderland	Sir Wm Chaytor & Co	1829	1836		
Sunderland see Darlington Bank	Backhouse & Co				

Bank or location	Firm or partnership	Founded	Issue ceased	Authorised circ.	Present connectio
Sunderland & Wermouth Bk.					
Suffolk Hadleigh Bank	Alexanders & Co.	1799			
Sussex & Horsham Bank	Blunt & Raper	1810	1816		
Swaffham & Norwich Bank	Day & Sons	1790	1825		
Tamworth Old Bank			1837		
Taunton	M & J Brickdale	1783	1816		
Taunton Bank	M & R Badcock Badcock & Co.	1777	1873	29799	Nat West
Tavistock Bank	Gill & Rindle Gill Moorshead & Co.	1790	1899	13421	Lloyds
Tees Bank (Stockton)	Thomas Hutchison & Co.	1785	1826		
Teignmouth Bank	Watts Whiteway & Co.	1840	1845		Lloyds
Tewkesbury Old Bank see Worcester Old Bank	Lichmore & Co.				
Thirsk	Fenton Scott & Co.	1793	1814		
Thirsk Bank	Britain & Co.	1822	1836		Midland
Thrapstone & Kettering Bank	Yorke & Eland Eland & Eland	1812	1888	11559	Barclays
Thornbury Bank	Ralph Yates & Parslaw Harwood & Co.	1808	1891	10026	Nat West
Tiverton Bank Tiverton & Devonshire Bank	Dunsford & Barne Dunsford & Co.	1788	1883	13470	Nat West
Tonbridge	Children & Co	1800	1813		
Tonbridge Old Bank	T W & S Beeching H S A T & A Beeching Hodgkins & Beeching	1815	1890	13183	Lloyds
Torbay Bank	Vivian & Co Vivian Kitson & Co.	1832	1900		Lloyds
Torquay Bank	Vivian Kitson & Co				
Torrington Bank	Loveband & Co		1843		Nat West
Totnes Bank	Prideaux & Bentall Wise Baker & Co.	1809	1833		Lloyds
Towcester Old Bank	J & S Percival Moxon & Percival	1800	1887	10801	Nat West

Bank or location	Firm or partnership	Founded	Issue ceased	Authorised circ.	Present connection
Town & County of Poole Bank — see Rigwood & Poole Bank					
Tring Bank Tring Bank & Chesham Bank	Butcher & Son	1836	1900	13531	Nat West
Tring Aylesbury & Chesham Bank			1840		
Truro	Praed & Co.	1800	1830		Lloyds
Tweed Bank (Berwick)	Batson & Co. Batson Berry Langhorn & Co.	1800	1841		
Tyne Bank	Baker Shafto Ormiston & Co.	1777	1816		
Union Bank (Cornwall)	Vivian Grylls Kendal & Co.	1788	1879	17003	
Uttoxeter	Bell Morley & Co.	1806	1830		
Uttoxeter Old Bank	Thomas Hart	1759	1846		
Uxbridge Bank Uxbridge Old Bank	Hull Smith & Co. Woodbridge Lacy Hartland Hibbert & Co.	1806	1900	25136	Barclays
Wallingford Bank	Wells Arnatt Wells & Co Hedges & Co. Hedges Wells & Co. Wells & Co.	1797	1905	17064	Lloyds
Walsall Old Bank	Charles Foster & Sons	1793	1848	19937	Midland
Ware	Dickinson & Co.	1808	1814		
Ware Bank see Hertford & Ware Bank	Adams & Co.				
Warminster & Wiltshire Bank	Morloch Everett & Co. Everett & Co. Everett Ravenhill & Co.	1760	1852	24896	Lloyds
Warwick	Whitehead & Co.	1821			
Warwick Old Bank	Dawes Jones & Russell Greenway Smith & Greenway	1791	1834		
Warwick & Warwickshire Bank	Kelynge Greenway & Co. Greenway Smith & Co.	1792	1887	30504	
Weald of Kent Bank (Cranbrook)	Wilmhurst & Co.	1804	1843		
Wear Bank (Sunderland)	Goodchild Jackson & Co.	1800	1815		

Bank or location	Firm or partnership	Founded	Issue ceased	Authorised circ.	Present connection
Wellingborough Bank	Molton & Roddick	1797	1825		
Wellington Bank	Fox Bros. Fox Fowler & Co.	1787	1921	6528	Lloyds
Wellington	Wood Carpenter & Co.	1805	1816		
Wells	Fuller & Co.	1808	1811		
Welshpool Bank see Shrewsbury & Welsh Pool Bank	Beck & Co.				
West of England Bank	Thomas Floud & Co.	1818	1829		
West Riding Bank	Leatham Tew & Co.	1801	1906	46158	Barclays
West Surrey Bank (Epsom)	Mangles Keen & Co.	1836	1864		
Western Bank (Exeter)					
Weymouth Old Bank	Eliot & Pearce Bower & Eliot	1791	1897	16461	Lloyds
Whitby	John & James Frankland Frankland & Wilkinson Chaytor Frankland & Co.	1778	1845		Midland
Whitby	Campion & Co.	1800	1841		
Whitby	Richardson & Co.	1786	1846	2076	
Whitby Bank Whitby Old Bank	Simpson Chapman & Co.	1785	1892	14258	Barclays
Whitchurch	Corser & Co.	1809	1828		
Whitchurch Old Bank	Trevor & Richards		1816		
Whitehaven	Johnston Adamson Hope & Co.	1806	1825		
Whitehaven	Moore Hamilton & Co. Hartley & Co.	1796	1824		
Wincanton Bank	U G & H Messiter	1800	1810		
Winchester Bank	Deans & Co.	1787			Nat West
Winchester Arlesford & Alton Bank	Bulpitt & Co. Bulpitt & Hall	1790	1892	25892	Nat West
Winchester & Hampshire Bank	Wickham & Co.	1807	1854	6737	Lloyds
Winchcombe Bank	Fisher & Ashmore	1797	1819		
Windsor	Brown & Coombs	1801	1816		

Bank or location	Firm or partnership	Founded	Issue ceased	Authorised circ.	Present connection
Windsor Bank	N Read & Co.	1780			Barclays
Wirkesworth Bank Wirkesworth Ashbourne Derbyshire Bank	Arkwright & Co. John Toplis	1829	1874	37602	Lloyds
Wisbech & Lincolnshire Bank	Gurneys & Co. Gurneys Birkbeck Barclay & Co,	1782	1896	59713	Barclays
Witham & Essex Bank see Colchester & Essex Bank	Mills & Co.				
Witney	Batt & Co.	1802	1815		
Witney Bank	Williams Clinch & Co.	1807			
Wiveliscombe Bank	W P & W Hancock W Hancock & Son	1803	1890	7602	Lloyds
Wolverhampton	R & H F Fryer R W Fryer	1807	1872	11867	Lloyds
Wolverhampton	Holyoak Goodrick & Co.	1816	1863	14180	Midland
Wolverhampton Bank	Gibbons & Co.	1782	1816		
Woodbridge	Brooke Riches & Collett	1797			
Woodbridge Bank	Alexander & Co. Dykes Alexander & Co.	1804			Barclays
Woodbridge & Suffolk Bk	Cooper & Alexander	1797	1805		
Woodstock	Cox Morrell & Co. Morrell & Co.	1818	1833		
Worcester	Farley Lavender & Co.	1794	1857	15463	
Worcester Old Bank	Berwick & Co. Berwick Richmond & Co. Berwick Lechmore & Co.	1772	1905	87448	Lloyds
Worcestershire Bank	Farley Turner & Co.	1793	1856	14309	
Workington	J & P Hodgson J Keys & Co. Bowes Hodgson & Co.	1802	1810		
Workington	Wood Smith Stein & Co.	1800	1812		
Wrexham Bank	Samuel Kendrick	1805	1848	3289	
Wrexham & North Wales Bank	R M Lloyd	1800	1840		
Wycombe	Thomas Edmonds	1808	1818		

Bank or location	Firm or partnership	Founded	Issue ceased	Authorised circ.	Present connectio
Yarmouth Norfolk & Suffolk Bank	Knowles Lacon & Co. Lacons Youell & Kemp	1791	1901	13229	Lloyds
Yarmouth & Suffolk Bank	Gurneys Turner & Co. Gurneys Birkbeck Barclay & Co	1781	1896	53060	Barclays
Yeovil Old Bank	E & J Batten J & H B Batten Daniell & Co.	1782	1849	10033	
York	Wentworth & Co.	1812	1825		
York Bank	Swann Clough & Co.	1771	1879	46387	
York & East Riding Bk	Beckett & Co.	1759	1920	53392	Nat West

JOINT STOCK BANKS OF ISSUE

Bank or location	Head Office	Founded	Issue ceased	Authorised circ.	Present connection
Bank of Westmorland	Kendal	1833	1893	12225	Midland
Barnsley Banking Company	Barnsley	1832	1897	9563	Midland
Bank of Manchester	Manchester	1829	1841		
Bank of Whitehaven	Whitehaven	1837	1916	32681	Nat West
Bilston District Banking Company — County of Stafford Bank	Wolverhampton	1836	1874	9418	Nat West
Birmingham Banking Company	Birmingham	1829	1840		
Birmingham & Midland Banking Company	Birmingham	1829	1840		Midland
Bradford Banking Company	Bradford	1827	1910	49292	Midland
Bradford Commercial Banking Company	Bradford	1833	1904	20084	Nat West
Burton Uttoxeter & Staffordshire Union Banking Co. — Burton Union Bank Ltd.	Burton-on-Trent	1839	1899	60701	Lloyds
Bury Banking Company	Bury	1836	1840		
Carlisle City & District Bank	Carlisle	1837	1896	19972	Midland
Carlisle & Cumberland Banking Company	Carlisle	1836	1911	25610	Barclays
Cheltenham & Gloucester Banking Company	Cheltenham	1836	1856	12786	
Chesterfield & North Derbyshire Banking Co.	Chesterfield	1834	1878	10421	
County of Gloucester Banking Company	Cheltenham	1836	1897	144352	Lloyds
County of Stafford Bank see Bilston District Banking Company					

Bank or location	Head Office	Founded	Issue ceased	Authorised circ.	Present connectio[n]
Coventry Union Banking Company	Atherstone	1836	1889	16251	Midland
Coventry & Warwickshire Banking Company	Coventry	1833	1879	28734	Lloyds
Cumberland Union Banking Company	Workington	1829	1901	35395	Midland
Darlington District Joint Stock Banking Company	Darlington	1831	1883	26134	Midland
Derby & Derbyshire Banking Company	Derby	1833	1898	20003	Nat West
Devon & Cornwall Banking Company	Plymouth	1832	1840		Lloyds
Dudley & West Bromwich Banking Company	Dudley	1833	1874	37696	Barclays
East of England Bank	Norwich	1836	1864	25025	
Gloucestershire Banking Company	Gloucester	1831	1885	155920	Lloyds
Halifax & Huddersfield Union Banking Company	Halifax	1836	1910	44137	Lloyds
Halifax Joint Stock Bank	Halifax	1829	1919	18534	Lloyds
Halifax Commercial Banking Company West Yorkshire Banking Company	Halifax	1836	1919	13733	Barclays
Hampshire Banking Company	Southampton	1834	1840		Lloyds
Helston Banking Company	Helston	1836	1876	1503	
Herefordshire Banking Company	Hereford	1836	1863	25047	Midland
Huddersfield Banking Company	Huddersfield	1827	1897	37354	Midland
Hull Banking Company	Hull	1833	1894	29333	Midland
Kingsbridge Joint Stock Bank		1841	1862	3952	
Knaresborough & Claro Banking Company	Knaresborough	1831	1903	28059	Nat West
Lancaster Banking Company	Lancaster	1826	1907	64311	Nat West
Leamington Priors & Warwickshire Banking Company	Leamington	1835	1889	13835	Midland

Bank or location	Head Office	Foun-ded	Issue ceased	Author-ised circ.	Present connection
Leeds Banking Company	Leeds	1832	1864	23076	
Leeds Commercial Banking Company	Leeds	1836	1846	13914	
Leeds & West Riding Banking Company	Leeds	1835	1846	18937	
Leicestershire Banking Company	Leicester	1829	1911	86060	Midland
Lincoln & Lindsey Banking Company	Lincoln	1833	1913	51620	Midland
Liverpool Commercial Banking Company	Liverpool	1832	1840		Barclays
Ludlow & Tenbury Bank	Ludlow	1840	1884	10215	Lloyds
Manchester & Liverpool District Banking Company	Manchester	1829	1834		
Manchester & Salford Banking Company	Manchester	1836	1840		Williams & Glyns
Mirfield & Huddersfield District Banking Company		1832	1836		
Moore & Robinsons Nottinghamshire Banking Compny	Nottingham	1836	1901	35813	Lloyds
National Provincial Bank of England	London	1833	1866	442371	Nat West
Newcastle Commercial Banking Company	Newcastle	1836	1840		
Newcastle, Shields & Sunderland Union Joint Stock Bank	Newcastle	1836	1847		
Newcastle-on-Tyne Joint Joint Stock Banking Company	Newcastle	1836	1846		
Norfolk & Norwich Banking Company		1826	1836		Barclays
North of England Joint Stock Banking Company	Newcastle	1832	1842		
North and South Wales Bank	Liverpool	1836	1908	63951	Midland
North Wilts Banking Company	Melksham	1835	1877	63939	Lloyds

Bank or location	Head Office	Founded	Issue ceased	Authorised circ.	Present connection
Northamptonshire Banking Company	Northampton	1836	1886	26411	Lloyds
Northamptonshire Union Bank	Northampton	1836	1919	84356	Nat West
Northumberland & Durham District Bank		1836	1840		
Nottingham & Nottinghamshire Banking Company	Nottingham	1834		29477	Nat West
Pares' Leicestershire Banking Company	Leicester	1836	1902	59300	Nat West
Portsmouth & South Hants Banking Company	Portsmouth	1839	1840		
Saddleworth Banking Company	Saddleworth	1833	1866	8122	
Sheffield Banking Company	Sheffield	1831	1905	35843	Nat West
Sheffield & Hallamshire Banking Company	Sheffield	1836	1913	23524	Midland
Sheffield & Retford Bank	Sheffield	1839	1848	18744	Midland
Sheffield & Rotherham Joint Stock Banking Company	Sheffield	1836	1907	52496	Williams & Glyns
Shropshire Banking Company	Shiffnal	1836	1874	47951	Lloyds
Stamford Spalding & Boston Banking Company	Stamford	1831	1907	55721	Barclays
Stockton & Durham County Banking Company	Stockton	1838	1846	8290	Nat West
Storey & Thomas' Banking Company	Shaftesbury	1840	1855	9714	Lloyds
Stourbridge & Kidderminster Banking Company	Kidderminster	1834	1880	56830	Midland
Stuckey's Banking Company Bristol Somersetshire Bank Somersetshire Bank	Bristol	1826	1909	356976	Nat West
Suffolk Banking Company		1842	1845	7449	
Swaledale & Wensleydale Banking Company	Richmond	1836	1899	54372	Barclays
Sunderland Joint Stock Banking Company	Sunderland	1836	1840		
Union Bank of Manchester	Manchester	1836	1840		Barclays

Bank or location	Head Office	Founded	Issue ceased	Authorised circ.	Present connection
Wakefield & Barnsley Union Bank — Wakefield Banking Company	Wakefield	1832	1906	14604	Barclays
Warwick & Leamington Banking Company	Warwick	1834	1866	37124	Lloyds
West of England & South Wales District Bank	Bristol	1834	1878	83535	
West Riding Union Banking Company Macclesfield & Huddersfield Banking Company	Huddersfield	1832	1902	34029	Nat West
West Yorkshire Banking Co. (see Halifax Joint Stock Bank)	Halifax				
Western District Joint Stock Banking Company		1836	1844	909	
Whitehaven Joint Stock Banking Company	Whitehaven	1837	1908	31916	Nat West
Whitechurch & Ellesmere Banking Company	Whitechurch	1840	1881	7475	
Wilts & Dorset Banking Company	Salisbury	1836	1914	76162	Lloyds
Wolverhampton & Staffordshire Banking Company	Wolverhampton	1832	1889	35378	Barclays
Worcester City & County Banking Company	Worcester	1840	1889	6848	Lloyds
York City & County Banking Company	York	1830	1909	94695	Midland
York Union Banking Company	York	1833	1902	71240	Barclays
Yorkshire Banking Company	Leeds	1843	1901	122532	Midland
Yorkshire Agricultural & Commercial Banking Company					
Yorkshire District Banking Company	Leeds	1834	1843		Midland